THE
BEAR RIVER
MASSACRE

BY COMMON CONSENT PRESS is a non-profit publisher dedicated to producing affordable, high-quality books that help define and shape the Latter-day Saint experience. BCC Press publishes books that address all aspects of Mormon life. Our mission includes finding manuscripts that will contribute to the lives of thoughtful Latter-day Saints, mentoring authors and nurturing projects to completion, and distributing important books to the Mormon audience at the lowest possible cost.

BEAR RIVER
MASSACRE
A SHOSHONE
HISTORY

DARREN PARRY

BCC PRESS

For information contact
By Common Consent Press
4062 S. Evelyn Dr.
Salt Lake City, UT 84124-2250

Cover design: D Christian Harrison
Book design: Andrew Heiss

www.bccpress.org
ISBN-13: 978-1-948218-20-7

10 9 8 7 6 5 4 3 2 1

CHAPTER 1

Mae Timbimboo Parry

It would be better not to know so many things,
then to know so many things that are not so.
—Felix Okoye

This is a deeply personal journey for me. My Native American culture has always been something that I was proud of, something that I wanted to share with the world. As a child, these thoughts and feelings were written upon my mind and witnessed by my soul daily through the hands and heart of a loving grandmother. I could talk for hours about those hands, which were always so soft despite years of bead work and tanning hides. Those hands also spent hours writing meticulously about her people, making sure that not one detail was missed. Her hands knew the meaning of hard work, taught to her as an Indigenous woman and deeply ingrained, like many of her habits. These hands would always come together at the end of the day to give thanks to Damma Appa, the Great Spirit who created us all.

I always knew that there was something different about her. She wasn't like other Grandmothers, who always seemed so *old*. She was quiet and thoughtful, but you could

Mae Timbimboo Parry beading moccassins, Clearfield, Utah

tell that she had an unbreakable spirit. I remember her black hair that lay wavy across her shoulders, easy yet strong, shining just as her soul did to me. Her dark skin, with its deep creases, told of a life lived hard; a life of giving; a life of loving and caring. This was my grandmother, my hero; this was my beautiful tribal elder who loved and served her people.

There was something about her small wooden home that made you want to be there constantly. It always seemed older than time, like the stories that she would share as she sat in her usual spot, at the end of the kitchen table with a pile of brilliantly colored beads. Grandmother would soon transform those beads into a beautiful necklace or adorn them on a pair of handstitched moccasins. Our people are known for their beautiful beadwork, with the Mountain Rose as our distinctive pattern. Her house had the comforting smell of smoked buckskin. I thought that all grandmothers' homes smelled this way, and it wasn't until later in life that I realized that wasn't so. Her mastered skills were carefully displayed on each pair of gloves or moccasins that were made; each bead threaded for someone she loved. For centuries, our people practiced those skills out of necessity. As I display these beautiful pieces of work in my home, I long to let her show me again how she beaded and tanned. Her strength and endurance shines through her art and designs and allows us to look back into her window.

She always had homemade stew on the stove with fresh bread nearby. I finally got the courage to ask her one day, "Grandma, why do you always have a pot of stew on the stove?" She taught me a beautiful lesson, one shared for many generations. She said, "In our culture you never have someone in your home without feeding them."

For hundreds of years, my grandmother's people were never more than a few days away from starvation. But the concept of sharing a meal or sharing what you had with a stranger was still deeply ingrained. Our people had no concept of personal property; taking care of our neighbors and their needs was a part of life.

I remember begging my parents to let me go stay with her. They knew how I loved her, and so they did. I spent almost every day of my youth at her side. We shared a special bond. I believe that she knew her journey to tell "Our Story" would one day become mine. Those carefree, easy days spent with my grandmother has given me a deep-seated understanding of her calling. Forty-five years later, I feel her influence and spirit daily as I have embarked on my own journey, though it is a path I never would have anticipated.

Mae Timbimboo Parry, Clearfield, Utah, ca. 1960

She was our storyteller, our tribal historian. The title is important to my Native people; the tribal historian makes sure our traditions and way of life carry on, with histories that have been passed down for generations. My grandmother remains with me now, though her body does not; there are times of each day when I feel her presence. Sometimes, when I am speaking with children about my culture and traditions, I feel her with me and hear her stories speak to me, like they did in my youth. I also feel her nearby when I meet people at the Bear River Massacre site who, like most people, are learning about the events of January 29, 1863 for the first time: the massacre of our people by the US Army stationed at Camp Douglas, in Salt Lake City. The Bear River Massacre was the largest massacre of Native peoples in the history of the United States, and yet it is largely forgotten. I felt her presence when I was negotiating for the purchase of that sacred massacre land, where more than 400 of our people died on that day.

It has taken me fifty-two years to realize how important my grandmother was in sharing our Shoshone culture and history. She set the record straight when it came to our Native American history, but it was also important to her that everyone's point of view was heard and respected. She would often say to me, "What is your story going to be?" She would call me to sit at her feet, just like she sat with her own grandparents, and listen to her tell stories. For hundreds of years, the stories were always the same, with never a word out of place. It had to be this way. It had to be accurate. If I was ever distracted or looked tired, she would stop. This was the only way that important events would become memory and be passed down to future generations. Have you ever had a memory sneak out of your eye and roll down your cheek? I have those all the time when I think about the stories she shared.

My grandmother was an educated woman. She was the product of the boarding school system of the 1920s, a system designed to assimilate the Natives into the Euro-American culture. Their creed was "kill the Indian to save the child." If she spoke her language or referred to her people or culture in any way, she was punished. The educational process was not easy on a young Shoshone girl. On one occasion while attending the Washakie Day School, her teacher made her stand on a chair in front of the other children and said, "Mae, you are going to turn out to be just like these other children, sitting in the dirt, and being useless for the rest of your life." But Grandmother was successful in school and in life. While in high school she did something that has literally saved our culture: she began writing down all the stories that she had heard from her tribal elders, and her grandfather Da-boo-zee, who took the name of Yeager upon his conversion into the Church of Jesus Christ of Latter-day Saints. Yeager was twelve years old at the time of the Bear River Massacre. We have a saying: "when an old Indian dies, a library burns." This was especially true about my grandmother Mae.

As I grew older and attended school, I developed a great love for history. I remembered the stories like "How the Coyote Stole Fire" and "How the Sun got its name," so I was eager to learn more about our people. It didn't take long for me to realize that none of the stories that my grandmother told me were in history books. At first, I was confused. I believed that historical events were an absolute. But now I realize that history is always about perspective. And then one day I read a quote attributed to Winston Churchill: "History is written by the victors." I guess that explains why Native American histories and perspectives have rarely been written.

I would like to change that. Our voices need to be heard, not because we as Native Americans are necessarily looking to have things made right (although that fight is an important one), but because those who died at Bear River have a God-given right to be heard. Their voices cry out to us from the dust. One of the most important statements that I can make as a Native American leader today is that "We are still here." We've contributed significantly to not only the United States, but to the world. There are not that many Indians in the US today, and we tend to get overlooked. Even when we are not overlooked, we are often misrepresented.

Mae Timbimboo Parry, Clearfield, Utah, ca. 2003

Our history books today are full of stories written from a single perspective. I find myself questioning what "different perspectives" might look like, because every day we have experiences that can be viewed from different directions. As you read about the Northwestern Shoshone Nation and Chief Sagwitch and others, as you read about the Bear River Massacre, my hope is you will come to realize that true knowledge comes as we learn to view the world from different perspectives.

You are about to read the story of my people, the Northwestern Band of the Shoshone Nation. Ours is a perspective that has never been written. The massacre at Bear River was the largest massacre of Native Americans by federal troops in the history of the United States. The ramifications were many. It changed how the US Army dealt with other Native American tribes in the future. The Army used the same tactics one year later at Sand Creek, attacking the tribe in their winter encampment in the early morning hours, when they were most vulnerable. It also permanently altered the lives of a small Band of people who only wanted to be left alone. The Bear River Massacre does not define us today. Our loss has made us stronger. We have used these stories and tragedies to inspire and motivate us to be better people and a better nation.

All of this brings me back to my grandmother. I have learned that people forget facts and figures, but they never forget how they feel when they hear a story. My grandmother was a storyteller, a calling that would one day be mine. Even when the effects of Parkinson's disease made it impossible for her to make gloves or moccasins, her mind was sharp and she never quit teaching. Now I share her stories with the world. My grandmother could only dream of once again owning the land that her people called home for hundreds of years. This has become a reality with the purchase of the massacre site. This sacred land and its history must be preserved.

I want to tell my grandmother that I am sorry for not paying more attention to what she was trying to teach me. I wish that I could go back and relive those days, soaking up as much knowledge as I could. I would write things down and commit them to memory, just as she always did. Every detail was important to her, a way instilled in her by her grandfather Yeager, as he learned from his grandfather. It was then, and is still today, the Indian way.

CHAPTER 2

My People

One day in my high school history class, the teacher started talking about my native culture. *Finally!* I thought, *I get to hear about things that had been taught to me by my grandmother.* I wondered whether my teacher's stories were going to be as exciting as hers. It didn't take long for me to realize that what was being taught about my people was nothing like what I had ever been taught by my grandmother. Not only were their facts inaccurate, but their stories didn't come to life like they did when I heard them from my grandmother or other tribal elders.

I feel like I was born about 150 years too late. Every day would be a new adventure with new conquests. I imagine myself sneaking around the woods and stalking big game, much like I do now. I like to tell myself that those qualities and traits are instinctive, but based on the number of animals I actually harvest with a bow, they are probably not. I often think about Sagwitch and my other relatives, especially when I am camping and sitting by a campfire. Time stands still when you are in nature with no cares of the world. Something about the natural heat and smell of campfire smoke soothes my soul.

I daydream about what the first white trappers and explorers must have thought as they came west and first encountered the great Shoshone people. Did our people seem different from other Native peoples that they met, or were all Natives the same in their eyes? Surely they noted how the Shoshone lived differently from the Plains tribes, whom early trappers would have met in Oklahoma and Nebraska on the way West. Our people are often referred to as Indians or American Indians, because the first Europeans thought they had found India. That term has stuck for centuries. While some Native Americans are okay with this title, many are not. [I use the word occasionally in this book not because I agree with the label, but because it is an aspect of the culture in which I was raised. It is part of my story.]

My friends in Archaeology and Anthropology at Utah State University tell me that the Shoshone are a Numic-speaking people, and that we migrated from Mexico more than 2,000 years ago. I don't know much about that; that ancient past seems far removed from my life. I do know that Sagwitch and his people lived like their ancestors did for hundreds of years. They were a proud people and only wanted what everyone else wants and strives for in this world—to be happy, to raise their families in love and peace. They wanted enough food so that their loved ones did not go hungry. They wanted to watch their grandchildren run wild through the forest like their ancestors had done for hundreds of years before them.

The great Shoshone people settled in the Western Plains and Great Basin areas. When they first encountered white explorers, the Shoshone numbered more than 70,000, extending from South Pass in Wyoming to the California-Nevada border. It was by far one of the largest tribes in the United States. By 1845, the Shoshone people was broken down into several large groups. The Eastern Band, under Chief Washakie, resided in the Wind River area of Wyoming, in what is Fort Washakie today. His Band numbered more than 2,000. In the Fort Hall area near Pocatello, Idaho, the Bannock Band of Shoshone numbered around 1,800 under the command of Chief Pocatello. Chief Tendoy led the Lemhi Shoshone of Central Idaho, who numbered around 2,000. The Northwestern Bands, referred to as the Snake Indians in some settlers' writings, numbered close to 3,000 and were under the leadership of Chiefs Sanpitch, Tosowitz, Ormshee, Lehi, Sagwitch and Bear Hunter.

Little Soldier led the Goshute Shoshone in the Tooele Valley and Deep Creek Mountain areas. Little Soldier became well-known for carrying a banner that reads, "The thousands of Manasseh," referring to one of the twelve tribes of Israel, in a Pioneer Day parade in Ogden, Utah. His participation in this parade is perhaps ironic, because he often had a very unfavorable disposition towards the Mormon pioneers.

Seven other Western Bands resided in Central Nevada and the Humboldt River areas, extending into eastern California, numbering more than 17,000 people.

Because of the vastness of their territory and diversity of landscapes, the Eastern Shoshone groups developed more of a Plains culture, with a primary source of food from hunting, particularly buffalo. The Western Bands developed a desert culture, relying more on gathering. Gatherers were always on the move as different food sources became available and in season. These Western Bands understood the delicate balance of nature and never harvested more than they needed. Tribes located in-between these regions developed aspects of both cultures. This was the life adopted by Sagwitch and his Northwestern Shoshone.

The Northwestern Shoshone were hunters and gatherers. We traveled with the changing seasons. We looked upon the earth as not just a place to live, but as our Mother, the provider of our livelihood and our very existence. The mountains, streams and plains stood forever, and the seasons walk around them annually. Our bodies were created from her dust; Blood that runs through our veins flows like the mountain streams from which it came. When it is time for our spirit to go home to the Father above the clouds, our bodies are laid down once again to the earth. Death was a beautiful concept to our people. If you lived a good life, then you are at peace at death.

Despite being one of the largest groups of Native people, little has been written about the great Shoshone Nation. Historian Brigham Madsen referred to our people as the "lost tribe," even though the Lewis and Clark expedition made the Lemhi Shoshone woman, Sacajawea, one of the most famous Native Americans in history.

I am often asked why the Bear River Massacre and the history of our people has been largely forgotten. There are many reasons why we have been excluded from history books. The history of the 19th century, like most history, has been written from the perspective of the victors. This alone would make sure that Native peoples' history and stories are never heard. Another reason could be that the pre-White West has been largely ignored by most historians. Civil war was raging in the South and East and very little news came out of the West. Our region was often

Newe (The People). Location and year unknown.
Photo courtesy of NWB Shoshone Tribal archives

thought of as an untamed wilderness, only occupied by the first peoples and the occasional adventurous trapper or miner. The railroad would change all of that.

My people, the Northwestern Shoshone, have always lived in Northern Utah and Southeastern Idaho, and particularly the Bear River Valley. They were nomadic gatherers, hunters and fishermen, traveling often into eastern and northern Nevada in the fall to harvest pine nuts. They traveled to central Idaho when salmon were plentiful, then to the Wind River area of Wyoming to hunt buffalo with Chief Washakie and their Shoshone cousins to the east. This was a happy season spent with family. Native peoples across this country still get together to renew family relationships, either in communal hunts or in sacred dances and ceremonies.

The old Shoshone used the expression *So-So-Goi* to describe themselves, which means "those that travel on foot." Before horses became available to the Northwestern

Shoshone, they used dogs and manpower to carry their belongings. They traveled hundreds of miles a year to different food sources in their annual cycle of food gathering. Small children learned at an early age that they were expected to share in the burden of moving, which cultivated not only a strong work ethic, but also showed what could be accomplished when everyone shares in the responsibility of caring for one another. Children were given small bundles to carry on their backs, just large enough for their physical abilities.

The Ute and Navajo frequently found their way into Northwestern Shoshone territory for trading purposes. The Utes traded their horses for Shoshone skins and pelts.

After horses became available, the travois was invented; long tepee poles that attach to each side of a horse. Mothers and grandmothers rode horseback and the children rode on top of the pile of goods on the travois. When the poles became shortened from being dragged, new poles were cut. Again, I find myself born 150 years too late. What young child wouldn't want the adventure of riding horses and riding atop the travois as they moved? I picture a child surveying the landscape, then jumping down to dart in and out of the sagebrush whenever a rabbit was spotted. Every day would have been a new adventure.

Because the climate and temperatures in the Shoshone homelands varied widely from season to season, our people made use of a variety of shelters. A travois could be used as tepee poles and moved at a moment's notice, while other forms were more permanent. The Northwestern Shoshone Indians made use of tepees, green houses and sometimes caves. Tepee covers were typically made from ten to twelve buffalo hides. The cover was stretched over twenty to twenty-five poles erected in a cone shape. Flaps around a smoke hole at the top regulated airflow according to the wind direction.

On the floor of the tepee were backrests and bed rolls. Items like clothing, medicine bags, shields, and other articles hung from the poles on the interior. Tepee hides were decorated with drawings of animals, birds or designs. Great dreams and acts of bravery were also remembered in drawings, like trophies for all to see—the Shoshone way of recording history.

The tepee was the lodging of choice during the long winter months, but were unbearably hot in the summer. Shoshone used structures they called green houses during the warmer months, made by fastening tree branches, leaves and other material to make a structure similar to the tepee with sides that allowed air to flow through. Green houses were typically left behind when the Shoshone moved on in the fall, though the structures could be moved if necessary.

Caves were an immovable part of the Shoshone landscape, used as shelter as members of the tribe traveled from area to area. They knew where caves were located and would plan on staying there when voyaging. Many of the caves in Sagwitch's travel area have significant rock writings inside them, telling the stories of those people.

A spiritual leader or medicine man would pray and dedicate a new dwelling. He would normally pray and do a smudging ceremony before the poles were covered. Smudging consists of burning sage, sweet grass or tobacco to cleanse or purify the surroundings. He would pray that the occupants would have a happy life together in the dwelling. He would pray that no evil would enter through the door opening, that the dwelling would always be open to the hungry, fatherless and aged. This is why my grandmother's home was always open.

The tepees were always furnished and made comfortable inside. Rabbit skin braided like rugs were made into quilts. Buffalo robes served as blankets, and sometimes as floor coverings. Dried moss blankets were not unusual. Woven sagebrush and juniper bark served as mats and mattresses along with boughs and cattail fluff. The Shoshone people were very good at weaving willows and sage brush and other natural resources. When the infantry from Camp Douglas attacked our people at Bear River, some soldiers remarked about the heavy dense fortifications that the Indians had erected near their dwellings. These were actually sagebrush wind breaks, carefully placed to block the cold Northern winds during winter.

Campsites were always erected in the same places at the same times of the year, in locations near fresh water and protected by trees, willows, shrubs or brush. Sagwitch knew what it meant to live in a dry and arid place, having experienced it as a young boy. Not only did Sagwitch know, but all Native peoples know and understand the delicate balance of living with nature. The sky, the earth and the water all play a pivotal role in not only Shoshone culture, but all Indian cultures. Not only does water sustain life, but to my people, water is sacred. Water is life.

I've been with my grandmother to many of the Shoshone springs, and the water is as clean and clear as it must have been in Sagwitch's time. One of my favorite places to go with my grandmother was to Conner Spring. This freshwater spring is located out in the Promontory area, in the Utah west desert, and served as a waypoint for travel to Eastern Nevada to harvest pine nuts or to go on an antelope hunt. They must have stayed for days at Conner Spring, because of many rock writings that can be found there today.

Because of how difficult it was to provide food for his following, Sagwitch and other Shoshone were not wasteful. They picked no more than was needed for their families. They killed just enough game for their family and any others in need at their camp, and when an animal was harvested, every part of the animal was used for food, clothing and shelter. Indians never killed game for recreation or for the pleasure of killing. My Shoshone people didn't have any concept of personal property, so everything was shared with those who had less. Every member of the tribe played an important role in the tribe's survival.

Indian women would socialize as they went in groups to gather seeds. Sagwitch's sisters would have accompanied their mother beginning at a very young age and begun to learn this important skill. Cradle boards would come in handy when a child was too young to participate, but would still go along—the board would be hung up in a nearby tree. The women took with them their tools of the trade: willow baskets, winnowing pans and hitting sticks. As they gathered sunflowers, wild rice and mustard, they told each other of the latest happenings in the camp. Sometimes they traded recipes and sang songs as they labored. Gathering was a hard task. When seeds were scarce, a mother might spend an entire day gathering enough for only one family meal. Digging sticks were used for digging roots and bulbs. Wild vegetables were normally plentiful, with a harvest of ground potatoes, camas, sego lily, wild garlic, cactus and other bulbs. Berries of all kinds were found in the mountains and fields, along with wild honey. Eggs were also gathered, a delicacy because they were so hard to find.

Meat was a central item in the Northwest Shoshone diet. In the fall, the men travelled into Western Wyoming and harvested buffalo and antelope, sun drying the meat for winter use. Deer, elk, moose and bighorn sheep were hunted in what is now Idaho and Utah. In Western Utah and Eastern Nevada, remnants of Shoshone sagebrush corrals could be seen as late as the 1930s. Hunters would drive deer or antelope in these corrals to facilitate their slaughter for food and clothing. Larger animals like moose and elk were much harder to kill, sometimes driving them over cliffs or chasing into large pits near watering holes to facilitate their taking. Rabbit hunting was done in the summer and winter months, and squirrels, wood chuck and other small animals were also harvested when found.

At different times of the year, fish were a vital part of the Shoshone diet. Our people would move into the area of Salmon, Idaho for the harvesting of fish, using spears, fishing poles and baskets as implements, and drying many of those fish for winter use. The Cache Valley was also an important place to fish. When the Mormon pioneers began to occupy the Bear Lake Valley in the early 1860s, they heard many stories from the Shoshone people

Shoshone women, Chon Zundel sewing buckskin gloves. ca. unknown, photo courtesy of NWB Shoshone Tribal Archives

about a monster that resided in the Bear Lake. My grandmother told me that a few Indian braves were fishing one evening on the lake and disappeared, and so the rumors began that a large monster had come out of the water and had taken those men. We were a very superstitious people! My grandmother then added that those men were probably drunk and had probably drowned.

Shoshone clothing was made primarily from tanned animal skins. Sagebrush and Juniper bark were also used. As many as seven hides from an antelope, three or four hides from a deer, or two large elk hides were required to make one dress. Dresses and suits were decorated with shells, claws and teeth from various animals. Bones and porcupine quills were also used as decorations. Sinew from animals was used for thread. Sagebrush and juniper bark were used to make capes, blouses and leg coverings.

Moccasins were made from deer, elk and moose hides, with rawhide the preferred material for soles. Rawhide soles are much longer wearing, and protect the feet when walking through rocks and rough places. Sometimes the moccasins were lined with juniper bark. As a young boy, my grandmother made me a new pair of moccasins every year. I still have them today. I also have a pair of gloves that my great grandfather, Moroni Timbimboo, made for me when I turned twelve. They look as new today as they did in 1972.

Head coverings or bonnets were made from animal skins. Lynx caps were made for younger children, with skin tanned very carefully so that when worn, the head covering looked like a natural Lynx. Bonnets were decorated with owl, hawk and eagle feathers. Eagles were considered the finest of all. Sometimes white weasel skins served as neckties.

A headdress known as a roach was traditionally worn by men and fancy dancers. This headdress was typically made primarily from porcupine hair, with a base made from deer hair. The winter hair of the deer was best to work with because it was longer and strong.

Wet clothing made from skins had to be removed quickly, then vigorously rubbed and stretched until dried to a soft condition. Wet moccasins would be worn until dry again to regain their softness.

Back then, marriage was arranged for nearly all. Sometimes a man would go to the home of a newborn's parents and ask permission to marry their daughter at some future date. If the parents liked the man and knew him to be a good provider, they would sometimes agree. Often, the parents refused this arrangement because they knew the man to be cruel or a poor provider or because they did not want to arrange for marriage so early.

In another approach to marriage, a man would send a gift to the girl's parents of a horse or several horses, or skins of all kinds, deer meat or other food supplies showing him to be a good provider. If the parents agreed, the marriage was arranged. This arrangement was not considered a purchase, but rather was considered compensation for the loss of services to her parents.

Sometimes to add interest to the marriage process, families would stage what we now call a tug of war. The bride to be dressed in well-made buckskin clothing that would not tear or fall apart. The mother of the girl and the mother-in-law-to-be would come together with the girl between them. Tugging on the girl would begin with the mother pulling one way and the mother-in-law pulling in the other direction. The winner was the one who pulled the girl across the line, and the girl had to go with the winner.

A marriage ceremony in the old days was conducted by the spiritual leader. He always gave the couple rules to live by, among which would be the injunction to be true to their mate at all times. They were counseled to be chaste in thought and to always remember their wedding vows. Sometimes the spiritual leader would pull hair from the bride and groom and tie it together. The tied hair was then taken by a relative to a hiding place only known to the relative—if later the couple wanted to divorce, they would first have to find the hair and untie it.

My Shoshone people lived a very complicated life. Nothing was ever given to them and nothing was ever taken for granted. Everything was done out of the necessity

Headdress of Chief Sagwitch passed down (Yeager, Moroni, Mae, Bruce) to great-great-great grandson Darren Parry. Photo 2019, courtesy of Darren Parry

to survive, and this is the only lifestyle they knew. This delicate balance of life was upset with the coming of the Mormon pioneers. The land that they had lived on for centuries was only able to sustain life for so many people. As more and more saints arrived in Shoshone lands, this would become an impossible situation for my people. The Pioneers had the ability and knowledge to plant and raise crops anywhere and at any time, technology unknown to Sagwitch and his people. They only knew one way to live, and in the end, it wasn't enough.

CHAPTER 3

Chief Sagwitch

I have been intimately acquainted with the white man from my childhood, and I appeal to any white man, when have I played false with him? Whom have I killed or even threatened to kill? I have ever been an advocate for peace. I abhor war today. I want peace. I sue for peace today. I want to be at peace with all men. . . . The white man roams the mountains all over, hunting for the gold and silver that belongs to the Indians until he sells the land. When have I interfered with him? The railroads pass through my country and have scared the game all away. Still I have made no objection to this, nor do I want to. I want all men to have the privilege of doing as they like, undisturbed, and make all the money they can, and all I want is peace and to be allowed to make a farm in a small, very small, portion of the country I have always lived in and still want to live in.[1]

—Sagwitch, August 31, 1875

One day, as I shared my Shoshone culture with a group of 2nd graders, a young girl asked me, "What do you have to

---

1 REFERENCE?

do to be Chief?" I had been introduced by her teacher as the "Chairman" of the Shoshone Nation, but the title of Chairman meant nothing to the young girl, so I told them that I was really "The Chief." A real live Indian Chief! Their eyes grew wide with wonder. The girl's simple question later made me reflect on what it means to be "The Chief."

In Shoshone culture, when a young boy or girl does an act of kindness or service, they are rewarded with a single eagle feather. As the boy or girl continues in a life filled with acts of courage, kindness and service, they are awarded more and more eagle feathers. When these young tribal members come of age, the Chief of the tribe assesses who among them has the most feathers, a sign of a life lived for others. A headdress is made from the eagle feathers, and that person is given a role of leadership. A Chief isn't the bravest, or the one who was most successful in waging war with other tribes or the white man, but the Chief is always one who has lived a life of service.

I often think about Sagwitch going through this same process as a young boy. I wonder what qualities made him stand out. He was a son, a brother, a husband, a grandfather, and he would become one of the leaders of the Northwestern Band of the Shoshone Nation. But he had a gentle demeanor, and a heart that was kind. It was no wonder that in 1856, Peter Maughan and the first group of Saints referred to Sagwitch and his Band as the friendly ones.[2] He was a friend and a provider to the early Mormon pioneers, when many in the region were not. He

---

2   Peter Maughan, "Incoming Correspondence: Peter Maughan to Brigham Young," February 3, 1862.

Chief Sagwitch, ca. unknown, location unknown.

was small in size, about 5′8″, but distinguished himself quickly in life as someone with unique potential. I believe that the Great Spirit sent Chief Sagwitch at that specific time to help his people navigate the waters of change that were coming for the Shoshone way of life, to play a role that would impact generations yet unborn.

When my grandmother spoke of Sagwitch, I could visualize the face and existence of someone that was incomparable. I am only just beginning to genuinely understand the depth of who he was. Sagwitch was born in the autumn of 1822, in what is now Box Elder County near the present-day city of Bear River, the son of Pin-en-netsi and Woo-rats-nats-in-gwip. His first rite of passage came at an early age: young Shoshone boys were stripped of their clothes, and rolled in the snow to determine their nature. Tradition declared that if a boy cried out, that child would grow up to be a coward, but if they endured this test well, they would grow up to be a great hunter and leader. Our oral history is that Sagwitch did not utter a word or cry out in any way. With growing age came additional responsibilities for this future Chief. He excelled at making bows and arrows, and became the tribe's best hunter and chief provider of food. Stories passed down maintain that his efforts saved his tribe from starvation on many occasions.

Sagwitch was a hunter and gather travelling with the changing seasons. His family was always on the move traveling with the changing seasons, a practice that led them to the most resource rich environment at the most opportune times. Sagwitch and his people were more fortunate than most and lived in the Bear River Valley and Cache Valley, fertile lands that provided abundant food sources. His winters there were always spent at Boa Ogoi, which in Shoshone translates into "Big River." The white settlers called it the Bear River.

Sagwitch was born at the beginning of the fur trading era. He never knew a life without the white man. From his youth he witnessed his people's interaction with mountain men and trappers as they bargained for goods and exchanged information. As he matured into the role of leader and chief, he developed a quiet confidence which promoted trust and understanding and made him persuasive in negotiations. In the Shoshone language, the name Sagwitch means "Orator." Sagwitch identified the power of the spoken word and relied on it as mediator for his people. A reporter from the Salt Lake Daily Herald in 1874 said this about the chief:

Chief Sagwitch & Bea-woa-chee (Bear Hunters widow) ca.1875–1880, Salt Lake City, Utah. LDS Church Archives, Salt Lake City, Utah.

A dark, heavy set, greasy-looking son of the mountains about 60 years old, and five feet eight inches in his moccasins. Of course, we who do not understand the languages, were not much edified by the speech, but the old man grew quite eloquent judging from his gestures, and actions, by the way, is about all there is of oratory.[3]

Sometime in the late 1830s, Sagwitch married his first wife. Her name was Egyptiitcheeadaday, which means "Coyote's niece." In the 1840s, he married his second wife, Hewechee, meaning "Morning Dove." Having more than one wife was common practice among the Shoshone.

---

3   Reporter, *Deseret Evening News*, September 15, 1875.

Only those men who were capable hunters and providers were given this opportunity. This was not a commandment from the Great Spirit as with the Mormons, but a necessity for those families that were fatherless. Sagwitch and his people took care of one another.

In the early summer of 1847, Sagwitch and other Utah tribes received word from a network of western tribes that a group of white settlers were making their way to the Salt Lake Valley. Encounters with the white man were not new to Sagwitch; many crossed Indian country in search of land and gold, though few stayed past the business of bargaining and trade. On July 31, 1847, Sagwitch and others traveled from the Ogden, Utah area to the Salt Lake Valley to greet Brigham Young and the very first contingent of Mormon pioneers.[4] Sagwitch's reasoning for the meeting was twofold; to offer peace and communications between the groups, and to determine stewardship over Shoshone land.

Because of illness, Brigham Young was unable to meet with Sagwitch, who instead met with Heber C. Kimball. Kimball immediately told the Shoshone leader that "the lands belonged to the Lord" and that the Mormons "calculated to plow and plant it."[5] This was probably not the beginning Sagwitch envisioned. It was customary for Sagwitch to meet with his counterpart in a respectful interaction; instead, he was dismissed and belittled for his gesture of good will. Unbeknownst to Sagwitch, this was just the beginning.

---

4   "The Pioneers of 1847," *The Historical Record* 9 (May 1890): 82–83.
5   Heber C. Kimball, "Journal History," August 1, 1847, 2.

Though their first encounter was foreboding, Sagwitch and his people continued to assist and interact with the Mormon pioneers as they settled the Salt Lake and Cache Valleys. For some time, the Mormon attitudes toward their new Native American neighbors were inclusive. To the Mormons, this group of people were the descendants of Lehi, a people known to them from their belief in the Book of Mormon. As more and more Saints relocated to the Utah territory, useful farmland became scarce, and Brigham Young sent scouts to find new areas for settlement. In 1855, he commissioned Peter Maughan and a small group of saints to settle Cache Valley, called Willow Valley at the time by early trappers.[6] This land was of vital importance to the Shoshone people, and more and more close interactions developed between the two very different groups. Initially their relations were peaceful and, on occasion, Peter Maughan referred to Sagwitch and his Band as "the friendly ones," stating "they have always been so since the settlement of this valley and we hope that they will continue their friendship."[7]

Other Shoshone Bands that frequented the Cache Valley were not so friendly and welcoming. Chiefs Bear Hunter and Pocatello were much more aggressive in their approach to the white settlers and those passing through on the California and Oregon trails. Still, Sagwitch and his Band continued in efforts of peace despite the

---

6   Mary Ann Weston Maughan, "Journal," in *Our Pioneer Heritage*, ed. Kate B. Carter, vol. 2 (Salt Lake City: Daughters of the Utah Pioneers, 1958).

7   Peter Maughan, "Incoming Correspondence: Peter Maughan to Brigham Young," February 3, 1862.

encroachment of settlers, in the belief that the adversity between the settlers and his people could be overcome. This tension between hope and unease would become the setting for the next few years.

Brigham Young had just led an expedition of Saints across the plains where many had died and others suffered hardships beyond imagination. He also had a book of scripture containing the dealings of Jesus Christ with aboriginal peoples of the American continent, written for these Lamanites (Indians) in our day and time. Even shaped by this knowledge, Young was confronted by the harsh realities of providing for his expanding group. How could he justify the removal of a covenant people according to the Book of Mormon, with whom he also had a divinely-revealed responsibility and charge to convert? Early efforts to coexist seemed to work, but the competition for limited resources would soon make this impossible. It is not without irony that these Mormons, who were pushed from their homelands as victims of hate, would soon do the same violence to others.

Sagwitch was well liked by the early Mormon settlers, who today lends his name to two mountain peaks and a basin in the Cache Valley. The goal of the Mormons was to forever establish themselves in Cache Valley. This place of beauty would become their new Zion. Finally perceiving this inevitability must have been painful for Chief Sagwitch. He had known the white man from his youth. The trappers and mountain men had always had temporary, transactional dealings with the Shoshone. But the Mormons were different. Now established, they would take hold of this land because it was the will of their God.

Descendants of Sagwitch gathered for dedication of grave marker. West of Washakie, Utah, May 25, 1963. Photo courtesy of Mae Timbimboo Parry.

Within seven years, Cache Valley would evolve from a place of cooperation to become the scene of the deadliest massacre of Native Americans in the Western United States. Henry Ballard, bishop of the Logan 2nd Ward, summed up the feelings of the Saints when he said,

> The Lord raised up his foe [referring to Colonel Patrick Connor, leader of the Army] to punish them [the Shoshone] without us having to do it. We have borne a great deal from them and still had been feeding them, yet some of the wicked spirits among them would stir up trouble against us.[8]

Anything can be justified in the name of religion. But despite the betrayal of the Mormons, Sagwitch possessed an internal strength and ability to forgive that has continued to save a nation.

---

8   Henry Ballard, "Journal," January 29, 1863.

CHAPTER 4

Patrick Edward Connor

I have heard his name often over the years and have seen images of him in my history books. I remember my Grandmother's sadness when my younger brother named his second son Connor. She had always referred to Colonel Patrick Edward Connor as a coward. As I have gotten older, I have started to understand my Grandmother's feelings. His story was deeply personal to her, as the man responsible for the most painful part of our Shoshone history. As our tribal historian Grandmother had to recount the story of the Bear River Massacre more times than I could count, each time a reminder of the person who was responsible.

Patrick Edward Connor was born in County Kerry, Ireland, on St. Patrick's Day, 1820. Life in Ireland in the early 19th century was difficult. Civil unrest and famine must have played a part in Patrick's decision to immigrate to America at age 19. I can't help but think of the similarities between his life and Chief Sagwitch, who was born only two years later. They both were born in rural settings and knew lives of scarcity. Growing up in that atmosphere must have made them deeply appreciate the simple meaningful things that life offers. Connor was largely able to escape his surroundings when he immigrated to America in 1839, but Sagwitch led the only

Brigadier General Patrick Edward Connor, ca. 1865, Salt Lake City, Utah. Photo courtesy of LDS Archives, Salt Lake City, Utah.

life that his people had lived for centuries. Their respective paths of escape and anchored tradition would bring them to a disastrous collision.

Connor enlisted in the US Army soon after his arrival in the United States on November 28, 1839.[1] This was probably an easy decision for Connor. The military provided him with a place to hang his hat, training and three square meals a day, a welcome refuge from his prior life of famine. He served as a "dragoon," mounted infantry who used the horse for mobility but dismounted during combat to fight on foot. His service took him to the Seminole Wars, Fort Leavenworth, Fort Atkinson and Fort Des Moines, were he was discharged as a private on November 28, 1844, exactly five years to the day of his enlistment.

1   Fred B. Rogers, *Soldiers of the Overland: Being Some Account of the Services of General Patrick Edward Connor & His Volunteers in the Old West* (San Francisco: Grabhorn Press, 1938), 91–92.

Fighting was now Connor's trained profession. He became a naturalized citizen on April 5, 1845 after moving to Texas, and in May 1846 he re-enlisted and joined the Texas Volunteers.[2] Connor would spend the next five years fighting in the Mexican-American War. Now a first lieutenant, Connor had the opportunity to lead other men into battle against aboriginal people. Connor was honorably discharged on May 24, 1847. Around this time, Sagwitch would be leading his people in an encounter with an outside force, with dramatically different tactics and tools at his disposal. Connor was killing Mexicans and Sagwitch was about to encounter Brigham Young and the Mormon Pioneers.

Patrick Connor was now living the life that would serve him over the next 25 years. In 1850, Connor moved from Texas to California following the discovery of gold. Many of those emigrants heading for the Gold Rush used the Oregon and California trails, which cut through the heart of Shoshone ancestral lands. Connor and Sagwitch were coming closer to the event that would define both of them for the rest of history.

On May 28, 1853 Connor was again called to serve his new country as part of the California State Rangers. His new job was one with which he was well-suited: to kill Mexicans, this time those considered outlaws by the state. He and the rest of the Rangers were well rewarded for their service by the state of California before the group was disbanded on August 29, 1853.

---

2   Spencer C. Tucker, ed., *The Encyclopedia of North American Indian Wars, 1607–1890: A Political, Social, and Military History* (Santa Barbara, CA: ABC-CLIO, 2011), 194.

Camp Douglas, Utah, ca 1866

When the Civil War broke out in 1861, Connor was in command of the "Stockton Blues" a unit in the California Militia. After increasing his unit to a regimental size, the group became the 3rd Regiment California Volunteer Infantry. Connor's first orders were to go the Utah Territory, protect overland routes from attacks by the Indians, and to quell a possible Mormon uprising. This must have been disappointing to Connor, who likely thought that his skills would best be at use fighting in the Civil War and not babysitting the Mormons.

In August 1862, Connor and his men established Camp Douglas in Salt Lake City, Utah. He became discontent with his assignment and longed to be back where the action was taking place. In correspondence to his friend, Major General Henry Halleck, Connor made the plea that he and his men had signed up to fight traitors, and they would be willing to give up more than $30,000 in pay to be transported back to the eastern battlefields. (His pleas were ignored, which probably added to his mounting frustration. In one letter to a superior in Washington, Connor wrote that the Mormons were a community of traitors, murderers, fanatics and whores. Not only did he not want to be there, Brigham Young and the Mormons did not want them there. They were trying, behind the scenes to get Connor and his forces removed through political channels in Washington D.C. with no success.[3]

Over the next three years Connor kept himself and his men busy. They established the first secular daily newspaper in Salt Lake, calling it the "Union Vedette." The paper offered a "gentile" balance in the news that was unavailable in the Church-owned Deseret News. Connor also took great pride in offering protection to those wishing to leave the Mormon church. His discovery of valuable minerals in the Utah Territory gradually brought non-Mormon emigrants to the region which also served to weaken the monopolist strength of the dominant Mormons.

In early 1863, Connor received word of attacks by Indians on the emigrants using the Oregon and California trails, as well as more minor acts of thievery and vandalism against the Mormon pioneers in the Cache Valley. This was now his chance to fight. Leaving Salt Lake City on January 24, 1863 under the cover of night, Connor and his men traveled 140 miles over four days towards the Shoshone encampment located on the Boa Ogoi. Chief Sagwitch and Conner were about to meet.

---

3   Rogers, *Soldiers of the Overland*, 91.

Connor and his men slaughtered what has been esti-
mated to be more than 400 Shoshone men, women and
children, the largest massacre of Native Americans in
the West, much larger than the horrors of Sand Creek,
Wounded Knee or Washita. In his final report to the Army,
he tabulated the Shoshone killed to be 224.[4] I interpret
this to mean that Connor only counted the men. He also
reported that seventeen men from his company had died.
The next day, three men from Franklin, William Head,
William Nelson and Willian Hull, went to the massacre
site at the request of church leadership and counted 400
dead.[5] Patrick Connor's reward for this victory was a pro-
motion to Brigadier General in the Volunteer Army. In
October that same year, Connor was instrumental in the
1863 signing of the treaty at Fort Bridger with the rest of
the Shoshone Bands.

Over the next couple of years, Connor continued his
slaughter of other tribes including the Sioux, Cheyenne
and Arapahoe. Connor's instructions to his men were
very clear: "You will not receive overtures of peace or
submission from Indians, but will attack and kill every
Indian over twelve years of age."[6] Much of the time

---

4   "The Fight with the Indians," *Deseret News*, February 11, 1863.
5   Daughters of the Utah Pioneers, *The Trail Blazer: History of the
Development of Southeastern Idaho* (Salt Lake City: Daughters of the
Utah Pioneers, 1930), 131; Newell Scheib Hart, *The Bear River Massacre:
Being a Complete Source Book and Story Book of the Genocidal Action Against
the Shoshones in 1863 —And of General P.E. Connor and How He Related to
and Dealt with Indians and Mormons on the Western Frontier* (Preston, ID:
Cache Valley Newsletter Publishing Company, 1983), 125–26.
6   Charles Griffin Coutant, *The History of Wyoming from the Earliest
Known Discoveries*, vol. 1 (Laramie, WY: Chaplin, Spafford & Mathison,
1899), 495.

Monument at Fort Douglas Cemetery, Salt Lake City, Utah, erected by the soldiers one year after the Massacre. Photo taken in 2019, courtesy of Darren Parry.

Connor and his men were on the defensive, fending off raids on their horses and supplies, which eventually left his troops on foot, wearing rags and reduced to eating horse meat.[7] On the whole, Connor's expeditions were considered a failure by the US Army, carried out by troops who only wanted to get home now that the Civil War was over. Patrick Edward Connor retired from active duty and went back to Salt Lake City, where he continued to pursue his mining interests and run his newspaper. He died in Salt Lake City in 1891 at the age of 71.

---

7   H. D. Hampton, "The Powder River Expedition 1865," *Montana: The Magazine of Western History* 14, no. 4, (Autumn 1964): 11.

Today at Camp Douglas you will find a statue, a cemetery with a monument, and a museum, all dedicated to honor Patrick Connor and his men and their legacy at Bear River. Unlike my grandmother, I will reserve judgement on Connor as a coward. I will let history speak for itself, and the Great Spirit will be his final judge. His life will be forever marked by the events of that fateful day in January. I abhor his actions at Bear River and will go to my grave believing that he could have done something different. Patrick Connor was, like any human, in many ways a product of his upbringing and lived the life he had been taught. He grew up believing that Native Americans were less than human, a rationalization that allowed him to carry out the atrocities for which he will ever be remembered. It is a painful part of our history. Connor's relatives and those ignorant of history may call him a hero. My Grandmother will always call him a coward. Regardless, our ability to learn from this event and others like it will determine our future as a people and nation, as both Americans and Shoshone.

CHAPTER 5

Massacre at Boa Ogoi

The campsite, in what today is Franklin, Idaho, was a natural, protected place, a perfect haven to spend the winter. The land along the Bear River a natural depression, thick with willows and other brush for shelter from the wind and winter blizzards. Natural hot springs nearby provided warm water for their daily use. This was the way that life was meant to be spent during the winter months: a time to reflect, renew friendships with loved ones and rest from all cares.

The area was centrally located in the Shoshone country, where the different Bands of Northwestern Shoshone gathered for meetings, winter sports and fun and games. They took part in foot races, horse races, played a game similar to hockey, and danced. In the winter, dried deer hides were used as sleds. In the summer, the children would dig foxholes along the banks of the river and play war. Over time, the foxholes got larger and deeper as the children played their games; it was later reported by the military and the white settlers from Franklin, that these children's play holes were rifle pits that had been quickly dug as defensive pits against Connor's soldiers, although this would have been impossible in the frozen ground of winter.[1]

---

1   "The Fight at Battle Creek," *Franklin County Citizen*, February 1, 1917

Highway 91, North of Preston, Idaho

Indians from the Eastern Shoshone Band near Fort Washakie, along with those from Pocatello's Band and Bear Hunters Band would assemble at the Franklin area with Sagwitch's Band for meetings and games. One such gathering was held in early January of 1863, an event known as the Warm Dance, a celebration to drive out the cold of winter and hasten the warmth of spring. If Colonel Connor had known of the Warm Dance custom, he could have killed thousands of Shoshone instead of merely hundreds.

Following the celebration of the Warm Dance and after all of the visiting Bands had left, Chiefs Sagwitch, Bear Hunter and Pocatello began settling into their normal routine. But trouble soon arose as a few Indians decided to steal some horses and cattle that belonged to the white settlers. The three men involved were One-eyed Tom, Zee-choo-chee (chipmunk) and Qua-ha-da-do-coo-wat (skinny antelope). They drove the animals out of their pen and headed north, killing one of the cattle for food along the way.

In retaliation for the death of four Shoshone men by Major Edward McGarry, A group of miners were attacked on December 8, 1863 and during that attack, John Henry Smith was killed. The remaining miners escaped to the nearby settlement of Richmond and eventually made their way to Salt Lake City to report the incident to local authorities.[2] The Indians involved were not from Sagwitch's Band, but Pocatello's, and the miners' horses and belongings were taken into Chief Pocatello's part of the country.

On November 25, 1863 in the Cache valley, another incident which the Indians believe served as pretense to their massacre was an attack by Indians that lead to the death of two White men. Two Indian men were also killed. This occurred on the road known as "Robbers Roost."[3] Again, the Indian men involved were not from the Northwestern Band, but to the white authorities and settlers, Indians were Indians and there was not much inclination to distinguish between the local natives and those from other Bands.

Because of fallout from these three events, many of the Indians were getting restless, concerned that trouble was brewing and that violence would soon break out. The settlers around Franklin began to call the Indians "stealing savages and beggars"—which was true from their perspective. Many of the Indians became bitter and

---

2   "More Indian Outrages," *Deseret News*, January 21, 1963; "Expedition for the Arrest of Indian Chiefs," *Deseret News*, January 28, 1863.

3   "More Indian Murders," *Deseret News*, December 17, 1862.

defensive, witnessing an encroachment of the White settlers into their lands and threatening their very existence. Many began to feel like trapped animals that would have to fight for their lives.

On the night of January 27, 1863, one of the elders of Sagwitch's Band named Tin Dup, foresaw the calamity which was about to take place. In a dream, he saw his people being killed by pony soldiers. He told those in his tribe about his dream and told them to move out of the area. "Do it now, tonight!," he said. There were approximately forty of Sagwitch's people that believed Tin Dup's dream and made their way to Promontory, thereby saving their lives.

Two days before the massacre, a white friend from Franklin came to Sagwitch and expressed concerns that settlers from the Cache Valley had made plans to get rid of the Northwestern Shoshones by sending an appeal to Colonel Connor to come and settle the Indian affairs once and for all. The Indians knew that Colonel Connor was coming; they did not know that the Colonel was coming to kill them all.

Chief Sagwitch, being an early riser, got up as usual on the morning of January 29, 1863. He left his tepee and stood outside surveying the area around the camp. The hills to the east of the camp were covered with a steaming mist, which seemed to creep lower down the hill. Sagwitch suddenly realized what was happening: the soldiers from Camp Douglas had arrived. The chief was not surprised. He started calling to the sleeping Indians, who woke, and quickly gathered their bows and arrows, tomahawks and a few rifles. Some of the Indians were so excited that they gathered up whatever was in sight to fight with. Some picked up their woven willow winnow pans and baskets and stuck their rifles through them. It appeared as though they had shields for protection.

Chief Sagwitch shouted to his people not to shoot first. He thought that perhaps this military man would be a wise man, who would ask for those responsible for the latest attacks on the white settlers, whom Sagwitch would turn over to the soldiers. He told his people to be brave and calm. Some of the Indians ran toward the river and dropped into the snow. They knew that they were not all guilty, but had no choice but to fight for their lives if attacked. Some had dropped into the children's play holes that had been dug along the riverbank.

Without so much as asking the Indians for the guilty party, the Colonel and his men began to fire on the Indians. Arrows were nothing compared to Army rifles. Indian men, women, children and babies were slaughtered like wild rabbits. Most of the violence took place along the river and among the willows.

According to the Indians, the massacre started early in the morning and lasted until the early afternoon. The Bear River, frozen solid in the morning, was now starting to flow. The Shoshone people were now jumping into the river and trying to escape by swimming across. The blazing white snow was brilliant red with blood. The willow trees that were used for protection were now bent down as if in defeat. The old dry leaves which had been clinging to the willows were flying through the air like whizzing bullets.

Ray Diamond, a nephew of Chief Sagwitch, was successful in his escape attempt. He swam across the river

Front - L to R : Angiechee (Survivor of Bear River Massacre in 1863), Mary Woonsook (daughter), Back L to R: Iva Eagle (grand daughter), Eva Wagon (great-great-great granddaughter), Eddie Wagon (great-great-great grandson). Logan, Utah, ca.

and found shelter away from the battle. He lived to be more than 100 years old. He told and retold the story of the Bear River massacre to the younger generations until the time he died.

Many Indian women also jumped into the river and swam with their babies on their backs. Most of them died. One Indian woman named Anzee-Chee was being chased by the soldiers. She jumped into the river and hid under an overhanging bank along with several other women. It was then that Anzee-Chee's baby started crying. In fear the baby would give their location, she chose to drown her own baby. By doing this they were all saved. She watched the battle from her hiding place, while trying to nurse the shoulder and breast wounds she had received. Anzee-Chee carried the scars for the rest of her life. She would often show them to the young Indian children as she told of the massacre of their people. She also told of losing her own small baby to the river. Another man swam with his buffalo robe upon his back. The soldiers shot at him, but their bullets did not penetrate the thick buffalo hide.

The soldiers first tried a frontal assault. The Shoshone shot and killed several soldiers, and continued with such aggression that the army had to fall back. As the army regrouped and began to flank the encampment, the Indians still alive were calling to their chief to escape so that he would be saved. Chief Sagwitch escaped with a wound in his hand, after having two horses shot from under him. Another Indian escaped by holding onto the tail of the horse Chief Sagwitch rode across the Bear River.

The cruelest killing was that of Chief Bear Hunter. It may have been the cruelest death in the entire struggle between Whites and Indians. Knowing that he was one of the leaders, the soldiers shot Bear Hunter; they whipped him, kicked him and tried several means of torture on him. Through all of this the old chief did not utter a word, because crying was the sign of a coward. Because he would not cry out for mercy, the soldiers became very angry. One of the military men took his rifle, stepped to a burning campfire and heated his bayonet until it was glowing red. He then ran the burning hot metal through the chief's head from ear to ear. Chief Bear Hunter went to his maker a man of honor. He left a wife and many children behind.

Yeager Timbimboo or Da-boo-zee (cottontail rabbit), a son of Chief Sagwitch, was about twelve years old and remembered the fight very well. He re-told the story several times a year and re-lived the scene in his memory. He told his story to friends, relatives and grandchildren until the story became imprinted on their minds. The grandchildren memorized the story and could repeat it by heart. Yeager told of feeling dazed and excited as any young boy would have during the fighting. He felt as if he were flying around. He dashed in and out among the whizzing bullets and was not hit. He heard cries of pain and saw death all around him. The little Indian boy kept running around until he came upon a little grass tepee that was so full of people that it was actually moving along the ground. Inside the grass hut Da-boo-zee found his grandmother, Que-he-gup. She suggested they go outside and lie among the dead. She feared the soldiers were going to set the tepee on fire at any moment. The boy obeyed and pretended to be dead. "Keep your eyes closed at all times," his grandmother whispered. "Maybe in this way our lives may be saved." Yeager Timbimboo and his grandmother lay on the frozen battlefield for what seemed like hours. Towards the end of the day, the soldiers were moving among the Indians in search of wounded to put out of their misery. Yeager, being a curious boy, wanted to watch the fighting once more. This nearly cost him his life. A soldier came upon him and saw that he was alive. The soldier stood over Yeager, his gun pointing at the young boy's head, but the soldier did not pull the trigger. A second time the soldier raised his rifle, and the little boy felt that his time to die was near, but again the soldier lowered his gun. The soldier then raised his gun for a third and final time, but as before, he lowered his rifle and then walked away. What went through this soldier's mind will likely never be known. Perhaps a power beyond our comprehension stopped this soldier from killing young Yeager so that the story of this massacre could be written. Later, Yeager Timbimboo would get the scolding of his young life. His grandmother reminded him that he was supposed to remain motionless at all times and to keep his eyes closed and to play dead. His disobedience nearly cost him his life.

Soquitch (lot of buffalo) Timbimboo, was at this time a grown man, the oldest of Chief Sagwitch's children. He would remember many things about the massacre. He escaped on a horse with his girlfriend behind him. Again, as bullets were flying in their direction as they tried to escape to the hills, one of the bullets found its mark and the Indian girl fell off the horse. She was dead. Soquitch kept going and reached safety. He dismounted his horse and sat down by an old cedar tree which was concealed by some brush. He proceeded to watch what the white settlers and Colonel Connor would call the Battle of Bear River. The little Indian camp was vanishing right before his eyes.

Toward evening, the field of massacre was silent, except for the cries from the wounded soldiers being carried away. The escaped surviving Shoshone people watched as the wagons left the camp. Blood could be seen along the trail they had left.

By nightfall the Indians who had escaped were cold, wet and hungry. There was no food, for the soldiers had done a good job of scattering the Shoshone provisions on the ground and setting fire to them. All of the tepees were burnt to the ground except one, which had been shredded to pieces resembling net. This was the tepee

Jane Hull - Sagwitch's infant daughter found after the massacre and hung in a cradleboard in a tree. Raised by the Hull Family from Franklin. ca. 1885

of Chief Sagwitch and his family. After the soldiers had left, Chief Sagwitch made his way to his tepee. He opened the flap and found his dead wife, laying next to an infant daughter who was still alive. Sagwitch gave the order to take the baby girl, put her into a cradle board (kono) and hang it on a branch of a nearby tree. He hoped that a kind-hearted settler would pick up the infant girl and raise her, knowing that without her mother's nourishment the baby girl would certainly die. Sagwitch's daughter was found by the Hull family from Franklin, Idaho. Jane Hull, as she was renamed, is buried today in the Hooper City Cemetery in Hooper, Utah.

Sagwitch was stunned. He stood idly and mournfully gazed at the scene. He remembered the many seasons the Northwestern Shoshones had spent in and around Battle Creek on the Bear River. He sighed and turned away. The bodies of dead Indians were everywhere. The survivors now realized that they could not hold proper burial rituals for the dead, so many were simply thrown into the river. A water burial was better than having animals eat their bodies. Chief Sagwitch ultimately realized that there were two different groups in his world. One group was greedy and wanted everything. The other group only wanted to live and travel around their land as they had done for centuries before. The first group made their wishes and dreams come true by making themselves the conqueror of the second, at the expense of a defenseless people who only wanted to be left alone.

As darkness fell upon the camp, a large fire was seen at a distance and a voice was heard saying, "If there are any more survivors, come over to my campfire and get dry and warm." The survivors gathered around the fire. Almost every one of them suffered from one or more wounds. Every man, woman and child were in a daze as they began to realize what had taken place. An old medicine man moved among the wounded and sick trying to heal them, but without much success.

Word of the massacre at Bear River spread quickly to other Indians. Some of the Northwestern Shoshones living in the Brigham City area heard about the massacre and decided to be messengers to other Northwestern Shoshone living near Promontory, Utah.

Two Shoshone women went into mourning for their dead friends and relatives. Poe-be-hup Moemberg and No-ya-gooch cut their long braids and slashed their arms and legs. They also tore their shirt sleeves and shawls, crying and wailing as long as they could. This practice was customary following a death.

The two women rode to Promontory to tell others of the massacre. Bleeding and weary, they reached the camp with their sad news. Tin Dup and his family and others that had evacuated following his dream had also just arrived. Their pack horses were still loaded down with their goods when the two grieving women rode into camp. Poe-be-hup quickly gathered everyone present and told them of the massacre that had just occurred. Upon hearing the news, Tin Dup took his rifle from his horse and then shot the horse dead. This was his way of showing his grief; he believed that his horse would be able to carry some of his people on their journey to the happy hunting grounds. The whole village then became a village of mourning, with crying and wailing for several days.

Fear of the dead was among the Shoshone people at this time; they feared that the dead would return to call the living. Mourners would practice ritual purification. A medicine man told the Band that they should be thankful for the snow that fell on the scene of the massacre, as the new snow covered the tracks left by the Indians who had escaped with their lives. The spirits are no longer walking the grounds of Mo-so-de-kane (home of the lungs), the medicine man said.

The massacre that took place that day has long been forgotten by most. I hope a new generation of people will have a desire to listen and to learn, not for vengeance, but because those who sacrificed so much speak to us from the dust, and we must listen.

Daughters of Utah Pioneers monument erected in 1932, Preston, Idaho. Photo taken in 2019 courtesy of Darren Parry.

If you visit the site at just the right time in the evening, you can sit and hear the cries of little ones calling for their mothers. Your senses tell you that you are among the spirits of more than 400 dead children of that Great Spirit who created us all. You don't have to see things as they were to know that a terrible injustice took place. You can feel it.

There is a plaque on the site today, erected in 1932 by the residents of Franklin County, that purports to recount the events of that fateful day. What the monument really accomplishes is to give people a reason to forget. Its self-justifying language strips us of our obligation to find out what actually took place, and it bitterly reminds us that history is written by the victorious.

The plaque reads:

Attacks by the Indians on the peaceful inhabitants in this vicinity led to the final battle here on January 29, 1863. The conflict occurred in deep snow and bitter cold. Scores of wounded and frozen soldiers were taken from the battlefield to the Latter Day Saint community of Franklin, Idaho. Here pioneer women, trained through trials and necessity of frontier living, accepted the responsibility of caring for the wounded until they could be removed to Camp Douglas, Utah. Two Indian women and their children, found alive after the encounter, were given homes in Franklin.

The problem with this narrative, besides its obvious lies, is that it only gives one perspective. It reinforces the view that the Indians were savages, and even went so far as to label our women and children as "enemy combatants." The plaque teaches that to the pioneer people, violence on the frontier was a necessity for the survival of Mormon communities, and it shows the consequences when whites and Indians had to share the same space. It legitimizes the use of violence if it meant that their communities would be safe.

What if the plaque had been written from the Northwestern Band's perspective? It might have said this:

The massacre of the Northwestern Shoshone Nation occurred in this vicinity on January 20, 1863. Colonel Patrick E. Connor led California Volunteers from Camp Douglas, Utah, and attacked a sleeping Indian village in the early morning hours of the day. The soldiers shot, raped, bludgeoned and bayoneted several

Edmond J. Fitzgerald mural, 1941, United States Post Office, Preston, Idaho.

hundred men, women and children to death. The Indians fought back with the limited weapons available to them, but the Band was all but annihilated.

So which version of the massacre is correct? I suppose it depends upon your perspective.

The massacre at Bear River was crucial to the history of Southern Idaho. It marked the closing of real conflict between the White Mormon pioneer settlers and the Indians in the territory. It allowed the settlers and farmers to encroach further into traditional Indian territory without fear. The US Army slaughtered nearly the entire Northwest Band because of trouble between a few Indians and the encroaching settlers. Patrick E. Connor was promoted to Brigadier General.

But this is not the end. Like all living and growing things, the Northwestern Shoshone people have sprung up from this humiliation and can hold their heads high, knowing that they are a part of the great American Indian Nation. We are determined to have our story told.

CHAPTER 6

Conversion

Once converted, the Lamanites will blossom as a rose.
Until that day the Indians must be embraced.
—Joseph Smith[1]

Native American religious practices and ceremonies can
vary widely and are based on the different beliefs and
experiences and the histories of each individual tribe.
These beliefs are commonly passed down in the form of
oral histories and stories taught to each member of the
tribe, starting at a young age.

Many of the tribes throughout the US focused their
religious beliefs around nature. Animals were symboli-
cally used to represent spirits and oft times used to tell the
story of the creation. As Christianity swept the country,
Native religious beliefs were misunderstood, dismissed,
and actively suppressed. This was probably made worse
by not having a written set of scripture or guidelines.
Just as the Preacher was to his white congregations, the

1 *Proclamation of the Twelve Apostles of the Church of Jesus Christ of Latter-
day Saints : to all the kings of the world; to the president of the United States of
America; to the governors of the several states; and to the rulers and people of all
nations*, New York, April 6, 1845, 3.

Shaman and Medicine Men and Women were to their Native peoples. They were leaders who communicated with the Great Spirit. These people were wise and carried with them a high level of status.

My Shoshone people also believed in spirits and powers that were centered in nature. The sun, moon, thunder and lightning and mythological figures like the coyote, wolf, rabbit and snake all played prominent roles in their religious beliefs. Shoshone shamans were also known as healers. These healers would place their hands on a person's body and exorcise the illness. The Shoshone people also used a wide variety of herbal remedies to cure illness with non-supernatural methods. Shamans also played an important role in communal hunts, for example antelope drives, where the Shaman would capture the antelope's soul through dreams, songs, and other ritual activities, charming the animals into the center of the corral, where they were killed.

This was the religion of Chief Sagwitch and his people. They had a deep faith that they could be healed by a greater power than their own. They would often be healed or blessed with what the Christian world would dismiss as crude or rudimentary rituals, like burning sage and spreading the smoke over your body in a practice known as smudging. My people never quarreled about religion or which church was right. They had always believed that the Great Spirit loves all of his children the same, and he is just as eager to bless them as he would be those who professed their belief in any organized religion.

For Sagwitch and his people, the principles and practices of Mormonism probably felt somewhat familiar.

Like the Mormons, Sagwitch and his people believed in spiritual leaders who were given certain powers to heal. They also believed in the laying on of hands for the healing of the sick or afflicted. They also believed in a God, or a Great Spirit who communicated to His people when needed, and they in turn, could communicate with Him through prayer. Those similarities probably played a role into the Shoshone people's later conversion to the Mormon Church. Or was the conversion of Chief Sagwitch and his Band, like many other Native Americans, an act of self-preservation? It might be a combination of both.

Even after Sagwitch and his Band were converted into Mormon Church, they still mixed their Native American beliefs and culture with Mormon doctrines. In one example, a Shoshone Mormon that went by the name of Ammon Pubigee told how his wife died, had a visionary experience, and then returned to life again. Her death vision included an expression of her people's belief in God and Christ, and instructed her on how to live on earth. She also continued to have other dreams and visions. This caused the people at Washakie to make her a beaded dress and saddle. The tribe would lead her on horseback around in a circle, asking for her story to be told over and over again. They believed that she had gained special spiritual powers as a result of her experience.[2] This practice probably worried the local church leaders, but not so much that they made them discontinue the practice (for a time anyway).

2   Charles E. Dibble, "The Mormon Mission to the Shoshoni Indians," *Utah Humanities Review* I, no. 3 (July 1947), 290.

Sagwitch experienced spiritual manifestations from time to time, but other Shoshone Chiefs and even other leaders of Tribal Nations also had similar manifestations.

A story is told among our people of an experience that Chief Washakie, one of the great Shoshone leaders of all time, had with a group of missionaries that Brigham Young sent to his people in 1856. Brigham Young had sent twenty-nine missionaries to find Washakie, who could be found near the Wind River Mountains. They were instructed to deliver to him a Book of Mormon and to marry the young native daughters when possible. This would help assimilate the Shoshone people and build bridges for later peace. Upon finding Washakie, they had a meeting in the Chief's tepee, presented Washakie with the book and explained its content and how the book came to be. The book was then passed around the circle many times as was a pipe. When they were finished, the Chief asked any of his counselors if they had anything to say. All of them spoke out in a negative manner towards the book saying that it was a book for the white man only. At the conclusion, the Chief grew quiet for a moment and then said:

> You are all blind and cannot see. The white man talks straight with us. He has told us that in not many winters the buffalo will all be gone and we need to learn a new life. We know this is true because our mothers and children are starving. There was a time when our Father who lived above the clouds loved our fathers who lived long ago. His face shone bright upon them and their skins were white like the white man. Then they were wise and wrote books and the Father above the clouds talked with them. But after a

while our people would not hear him and they quarreled and stole and fought until the Great Father got mad and turned his back on them. By doing this He caused a shade to come over them and their skins turned black. And now we cannot see as the white man sees, because the Great Fathers face is towards him and His back is towards us. But after a while the Great Father will quit being mad and He will turn his face towards us. Then our skins will become white.

A story similar to this can be found in the Book of Mormon, a book that Washakie had never before encountered.

Sagwitch and his people were now entering a very different phase of life. I would like to think that they enjoyed living the only life they had ever known. Continuing expansion within the Mormon communities pushed Sagwitch and his people away from hunting and gathering toward adapting a more Anglo-agricultural lifestyle. One could speculate that this was a contributing factor for Sagwitch and his people to be open to a different way of life for their very survival. This change toward cultural assimilation along with Chief Sagwitch's own spiritual manifestations brought him to the doorstep of George Washington Hill, the man most instrumental in the conversion of Sagwitch to the Mormon faith.

George Washington Hill was born on March 5, 1822, in Federal Creek, Ohio, into a Methodist family. George would be baptized a Mormon after marrying Cynthia Stewart (herself a member of the faith) and moving to Winter Quarters in February 1846. Hill was asked to stay behind when the first group of Mormons headed west, and to help organize the next group of saints which would

George Washington Hill, ca. 1875. Known by the Shoshone as Inkapompy, "Man with Red Hair." Copy photograph courtesy LDS Church Archives, Salt Lake City.

start their journey a few months later. George and Cynthia arrived in the Salt Lake Valley on September 18, 1847, two years to the day after the couple had wed. Upon their arrival, the Stewart and Hill families were assigned by Brigham Young to travel north and establish themselves in what would become Ogden, Utah. Ogden was also then the home of Chief Sagwitch and the Northwestern Band of the Shoshone Nation.

George Washington Hill was not a stranger to other Native Americans and their customs. He had a calm, confident demeanor with a certain strength that served him well. To Indian leaders, those attributes were celebrated and respected, and enabled him and his party to negotiate their way out of trouble. Because of his strength and confidence in dealing with Native people as he traveled across the plains, and later with the Shoshone he encountered in the Ogden area, George soon became a friend to this people and was known as someone that they trust.

In April 1855, George and his family traveled to Salt Lake City and attended the General Conference of the church. At the conclusion of this conference, George received a calling from Brigham Young to serve a mission to the Lamanites in the Northern country, lands now located in the Salmon River area of Idaho and the area of Fort Hall, Idaho. I am sure that there was some apprehension when George accepted this calling. He now had three small children. Hill didn't know the Shoshone language, and the thought of leaving his wife to fend for the family must have been terrifying. But George and Cynthia had an unbelievable amount of faith that the Lord would provide. When George was set apart for this mission, he was promised that the Indians would be hungry to hear the message, and be able to understand him, and come to him by the hundreds to be baptized. George could not then have known, but would come to realize much later, that his mission would change the lives of not just hundreds, but thousands of people.

Today the Portneuf River runs lazily through the city of Pocatello, Idaho. In the summer of 1855, George Washington Hill and his missionary companions camped for a night on a bluff about five miles south of the modern-day city. In the morning, as they prepared for their day's travels, they looked north and hundreds of Indians on horseback making their way to their camp. George then made a prophetic statement and said, "These are some of my children and I am going to baptize them." After a warm greeting by the two groups, the chief told George that the Great Spirit had told them of their coming and they were prepared to hear their words.

George and his companions must have been ecstatic as they heard those words. George brought out a copy of the Book of Mormon and told them that this book contained a history of their forefathers. He told them that many years ago the Great Spirit had visited the earth and had died for them and that he also visited their forefathers in this land. He told them that while the Great Spirit was here, he performed many miracles by healing the sick, lame and blind, and had power over the elements. He told the chief and his people that the Great Spirit had given His power to a man that lived on the earth today, that he had set up a church, and in order to become part of the church they needed to be baptized. With one voice the Indians raised their hands and said that they wanted to be baptized—and so they were. George's mind must have wandered back to the blessing he had received when he was set apart as a missionary and was promised that the Lamanite people would come by the hundreds to hear his words and be baptized.

Before leaving the Indians at Fort Hall, the local Shoshones gave George an Indian name that he carried for the rest of his life. They called him Inka-Pompy, which translated means man with red hair and beard. Giving George an Indian name was a sign of respect and love, and they hated to see him go. He and his two missionary companions headed north into central Idaho, just north of the Salmon River, and there met a Band of Bannock Indians. Their chief greeted the missionaries warmly and expressed gratitude for them coming. Like the chief at Fort Hall, the Bannock chief told Inka-Pompy that the Great Spirit had told them of his coming. The missionaries constructed a small fort and began to teach the Bannock and local Nez Perce the gospel of Jesus Christ. On many occasions they performed blessings and healings with those that were brought before them, and hundreds were baptized over the next few months. In the end, only George did the baptizing; the two other missionaries that accompanied Inka-Pompy never learned the Indian language, and as a result never did any of the teaching. Inka-Pompy had developed a great love for these children of the forest, and that love was returned tenfold.

George overheard the Indians talking about an Indian prophet who would visit them in their time of need. They told them of his sudden and mysterious appearances and disappearances. On one occasion, this Indian prophet was sitting in a tepee surrounded by Indians, and he was prophesying of things which should soon happen to them, when all of a sudden he stopped mid-sentence and remarked, "Some of my people are in trouble." He named a place that was about twenty miles to the south of their location. He stood, remarked that he must go and help them out, and left the tepee. Some of the men rose to follow him but could see no sign of him. He had disappeared. Hill interpreted this to be one of the Three Nephites which had a profound impact on him and strengthened his testimony of the work he was doing.

George returned home later that year and was released from his mission. He was successful in bringing the gospel of Jesus Christ to hundreds. His name in Indian country was held with the highest esteem. He was a father figure to all he taught and met. George planted crops, and took a job as a night watchman for the Union Pacific Railroad.

Some fifteen years passed, and George was well known in the Ogden area and served as a leader among his own people. George built a second home on his property where his Indian brothers and sisters could stay as they came to visit, which they did with some frequency.

In the early spring of 1873, Chief Sagwitch had a dream while sleeping in his tepee. Three men appeared to Sagwitch and told him of the existence of a God or Great Spirit among the Mormon people. He was told that this God was a true God and they needed to be taught about Him. The old Chief was told that they needed to change their roaming ways and learn to live as their Mormon neighbors were living.

The next morning, Sagwitch arose and made his way from his camp site just north of Corrine, Utah to Ogden to speak with Inka-Pompy. I am convinced that the two knew each other well, although Sagwitch had never been taught Mormon doctrines. When he arrived at Hill's home, Sagwitch knocked on the door and was greeted by Cynthia. He told her that he needed to speak to Inka-Pompy immediately. She told the old chief that he had worked all night and he needed to sleep in the day. According to Cynthia, Sagwitch was very disappointed, but he did not leave. He went out into the yard, sat on a log and waited most of the day until George appeared. Sagwitch excitedly approached George and told him that messengers had visited him in the night and told him that he needed to be taught to be a Mormon. George told Sagwitch that he couldn't teach and baptize him, because he was no longer a missionary. Sagwitch asked him if he still had special power to baptize, and was told that he did, but there was an orderly way in the church, and he must be given a special assignment by the prophet to teach and baptize.

Sagwitch went away, but came back the next morning and repeated the same process. He knocked on the door and was again told by Cynthia that George was asleep and that she would not wake him up. The old Chief also did what he had done the day before: he went and sat on the same log and waited for Inka-Pompy. I imagine that they had the same conversation that had taken place the day before, resulting in Sagwitch going away disappointed and probably a little bit frustrated. How could messengers appear to him and tell him about a God among the Mormon people, only to find that path closed to him??

The next day, George received a letter from Brigham Young, asking that Hill come to his Salt Lake office. George boarded the 5:00 train that afternoon and traveled to Salt Lake. Brigham Young told George that he had an important assignment; that that a great load had been resting on his shoulders for some time, and that this was now going to be George's load. He told George that he wanted him to take charge of a mission to the local Indians in the North Country; that they needed to be taught and baptized; that they needed to have land that they could call their own, and learn to till and plant crops and become a productive people. George was counselled to seek the Lord in prayer for guidance, and told that if he needed further counsel, Young's office was always open—but this was all his burden now.

Not long after George had visited with Brigham Young, Sagwitch once again appeared early in the morning at the doorstep of the Hill home. As usual, Cynthia told Sagwitch that George was still sleeping, and that he could speak to him when he was awake. Sagwitch waited in his usual spot, but this time he did not go away disappointed. Sagwitch again made the request for George to come and teach his people. He reiterated that the Great Spirit had told him that he would come and teach them all that they needed to know to be baptized. Inka-Pompy then responded, "Yes Chief, I will come. The Great Spirit told our Prophet to send me to you. I will come, but I can't come today. You will have to wait until I can come. Maybe a day, maybe a week, maybe a month, but I will come." Sagwitch felt unbelievable joy as he finally received his answer.

George went to work again that night, but when he arrived at the train station, he was informed that there had been an accident at Evanston, Wyoming, and that no trains would be coming from the East. With no work to do, and with very little thought or planning, George jumped on a freight train headed North to Corrine. He arrived just before daybreak and waited until it was light to survey his surroundings.

Sagwitch and his Band were camped about fifteen miles north of Corrine, and George took out on foot to find his soon-to-be new congregation. About one mile outside of Corrine, George encountered a young Indian brave on horseback headed for town. The brave smiled at Inka-Pompy, and said that everyone was waiting for him and that he was headed to town to acquire some meat for the feast. George must have been puzzled by this, as he had clearly told the Chief that he would be coming at some point in the weeks and months to come. George continued on, and two or three miles later encountered another

Indian boy on horseback, headed for town to buy some more food. He also excitedly greeted Inka-Pompy, and told George that his people were cleaning up the camp site and putting on their best clothes as they waited for his arrival. What George did not know was that when Sagwitch had returned home after talking to George, he had another dream. In this dream, Sagwitch was told by the Great Spirit that Inka-Pompy would be coming that very next morning and that he needed to prepare his people.

As George walked towards the Shoshone camp site, he could see in the distance someone riding on a horse and leading an extra horse. It was Chief Sagwitch. Sagwitch greeted his friend and told him that the Great Spirit had informed him of coming; he could see him from a great distance and thought that he would be tired. After arriving at camp, they all sat down to a fine Indian breakfast. The leaders both knew it was important to meet physical needs before you can be spiritually fed. What was not lost on George was the fact that the Great Spirit had arranged for this meeting; the spirit had whispered to Sagwitch many times and he listened; the spirit had made it possible for Brigham Young to transfer a "heavy load" upon George's shoulder. Hill prepared his whole life to serve a group that desperately needed guidance now that their world had been tipped upside down.

After breakfast, the Chief assembled his small Band in a circle, and George began to teach them the gospel of Jesus Christ. He taught them Mormon church doctrines about where they had come from, and what happens after death. Inka-Pompy told them of the golden plates that had been given to Joseph Smith by one of their ancient

C.C. Christensen 1871 panorama used to teach Native Americans the gospel

brothers. The plates contained the stories of their ancestors, George said, and told how the Great Spirit would
want them to live in today's world. When George finished preaching, he baptized Sagwitch and 101 others on
May 3, 1873. They were baptized in the Bear River.

Five days later, Sagwitch travelled to Salt Lake City and
met with Demick B. Huntington, who was currently serving
as the Patriarch for the Salt Lake Utah Stake. Huntington
was also a leading Indian interpreter in early Utah territory. Brother Huntington conferred the Melchizedek
Priesthood upon Chief Sagwitch, and ordained him an
Elder. This was a special honor and privilege for Sagwitch,
who had always been a leader to his people, but now had,
according to Mormon belief, the same power that Jesus
Christ had while he performed his ministry and miracles

on earth. What new opportunities would this bring to Sagwitch and his people?

For the next few years, Sagwitch's Band was incredibly dedicated and devoted to this new religion. They showed powerful faith and belief, which they perceived as the same God that the Shoshone people had always known and trusted in. As new converts there was much to learn and do, as they tried to learn a new way. For many years the whole community were full tithing payers, willingly giving 10% of their increase to the church for those in need. This period recalls the story of the "widow's mite" in Mark 12; the new converts possessed very little, but still gave everything that they had out of faith. Most of the children born at this time were given names from the Book of Mormon such as Ammon, Moroni, Lehi or Nephi. My great grandfather was Moroni Timbimboo, and all nine of his brothers were named after Book of Mormon prophets.

When the Logan Temple was under construction, my people donated more than 1,000 hours to building the House of the Lord. The men from Washakie would walk forty-five miles to the temple site and work all week, before walking back home for the weekends. I spoke in Logan some time ago at a single adult fireside. An elderly woman approached me before the program began, and gave me a brown paper sack. In it were an old pair of worn beaded buckskin gloves that had been given to her grandmother when she was a young girl. Their family lived next to the Logan temple, and the mother would make the Indian men fresh bread every day that this young girl would deliver. One day as she delivered the bread, an old

Shoshone Indians on Logan Tabernacle Grounds, 1909. Photo courtesy of Mae Timbimboo Parry.

Indian by the name of Grouse Creek Jack presented this girl with those beaded gloves. Those old worn gloves represent a spirit of service and giving, the same principles taught in the Mormon temple to Sagwitch and his people.

Not only did they help build the temple, but my people were faithful in going often to the temple, where they performed vicarious rites for their ancestors who lost their lives at Bear River. Sagwitch and his Band participate in the temple dedication. They were even permitted to put their tepees on the temple grounds, and participated in a parade through Logan as part of the celebration. On May 23, 1875, Sagwitch and his fifth wife, Bee-woo-chee, were one of the first "Lamanite" couples to go through the Endowment House and were sealed as husband and wife for time and eternity by Wilford Woodruff.

Washakie Farms was established in 1880 by the Church for the settlement of the Northwestern Shoshone. It is located just south of Portage, Utah in the far Northern Box Elder County. After the church was established at Washakie, the Indians began to fill local leadership positions within the church. Sagwitch's grandson Moroni Timbimboo, my great-grandfather, was called to be the first Lamanite Bishop. Both of his counselors were Shoshone. Sagwitch's young son Be-shup, who survived the massacre at Bear River and was later sold to a pioneer family and went by the name of Frank Timbimboo Warner, was called to be the first Lamanite missionary. He went on to serve three missions. He set the example for many more to follow. This was only the beginning for a people who had embraced a new way of life.

Because they originally had no concept of personal property, the Shoshone were successful for a time in living the United Order at the Washakie Farm. This order meant that the people had all things in common. They were a virtuous and pure-hearted people who took care of one another. They were now ready to navigate the long road ahead of them. The Shoshone were now prepared with a new religion, a new adopted culture, and principles that would serve them for generations.

CHAPTER 7

Way to Washakie

The Shoshone Indian settlement known as Washakie has
long enjoyed the distinction of being one of the few Utah
Indian communities not located on a Federal Reservation.
Not being on reservation land has proved a tremendous
blessing to my Northwestern Band of Shoshone Nation,
but the pathway has not always been easy. Stories shared
by my grandmother Mae tell of loyal friendships, disappointing betrayals and continued perseverance.

Our people were scattered after the massacre at Bear
River. Some of our Band made their way north to the Fort
Hall Indian Reservation, and some travelled east to the
Wind River Reservation in Wyoming. Others tried to settle in Brigham City and Promontory, Utah. My people's
traditional nomadic way of life was over. The ancient
grounds where they had hunted and gathered were lost
to them through the encroachment of the Mormon pioneers and other settlers. Though beaten and somewhat
disorganized, the tribal members still had to survive
with increasingly limited resources. Further interactions
between Chief Sagwitch and local settlers became inev-
itable. These dynamics, along with Sagwitch's spiritual
promptings directed the path forward for the Band.

Band In the year following his conversion, Sagwitch
sought the aid of a trusted advisor by the name of John

Moemberg. Moemberg was not only a friend to the Chief, but a tribal leader and cousin by blood. During the massacre, John was working and living in the Brigham City area and thus escaped. He had learned the English language while working for white farmers in Box Elder County, and served as Sagwitch's interpreter. While camped in Cache Valley in 1874, Chief Sagwitch, John and several Indians within the remaining Band came to a conclusion: to survive as a people, their only recourse was to attempt to take up land and begin farming like the white settlers. They decided to get a message to President Brigham Young and ask him for his help in this endeavor. Sagwitch and John then traveled to Wellsville in Cache Valley to seek the help of Frank Gunnell, a man known as a true friend to the Indians. Gunnell wrote a letter to Brigham Young on their behalf concerning their request. In response to the letter, Brigham Young commissioned George Washington Hill once again to visit the Indians and see how he could best direct them.

Mr. Hill suggested Franklin, Idaho as a place for their new home. This was welcome news to Sagwitch, as he and his Band had lived in that area in the past; they were very familiar with its surroundings and had wintered there for many seasons. Once in Franklin, they were introduced to Mr. Lorenzo Hill Hatch, a Mormon Bishop who helped them locate a suitable piece of ground and directed them to odd jobs. They cut down trees for firewood, haul loads from the canyon into town and worked as farm hands. They also helped build the road up the Maple Creek Canyon near Franklin. But though the Indians were no strangers to hard work, being bossed around by the white man was a new concept. Often the Indians were only paid through food and supplies—little help in developing new areas of land. After numerous complaints from the tribe, Chief Sagwitch held a council and the decision was made to move again. As thousands of years of tradition had instilled in them, the Band knew they could travel elsewhere to survive.

They devised a plan on how they could be paid for all the work they had provided to the community. The Band invited the whole town for a dance and celebration show. White farmers and settlers came by wagon with their families from all areas of Franklin to see the big Indian show. The Indians spoke in the Shoshone language and laughed and danced for hours in a wonderful representation of their culture. At the conclusion, baskets were passed among the crowd for donations from those in attendance. The event was a massive success. Though this was something to celebrate, the Shoshone had once again become landless Indians. The attempt to establish a community in Franklin, Idaho proved thankless and ungratifying. As George Washington Hill continued in his duty to locate a more permanent establishment for the converts, Sagwitch and his Band would soon look to Corrine, Utah.

Corrine was located just west of Brigham City and was occupied with people of all colors. This was a true Wild West railroad town, a melting pot for many nationalities. Corrine was referred to as the "Gentile City" by the Mormons and lived up to this reputation: here, the Shoshone met Chinese railroad workers, Irish rail workers, Mexican laborers, farmers, and ordinary lazy

Shoshone Indians at Corinne, Utah, ca. 1870

whiskey drinkers. The Shoshone were especially fas-
cinated with the Chinese workers and their incredible
industriousness. They saw tent cities that moved along
with the tracks being laid by the railroad, and also met
friendly white people willing to share with them their
knowledge of farming.

George Washington Hill located a promising area just
five miles outside of Corrine. As Chief Sagwitch held
council, it was decided that they would try to camp and
farm near Corrine. The Northwestern Band of Shoshone
became Hill's core group on the new Indian Farm. The
Band purchased a small farming plow, and planted
crops and were looking forward to new beginnings as
they adapted to this white way of life. Word quickly
spread through the native population of the success and
well-being of the Mormon natives on the farm.

A reporter from the Deseret News, July 22, 1875 published the following:

Civilization among the Indians

Yesterday we met with Brother George W. Hill who had charge of a colony of several hundred Indians, mostly of the Shoshone and Bannock Tribes. They are Indians who have come forward and asked to be baptized. The location is in Bear River Valley, Utah territory, and quite a breadth of land has been farmed by them during the past season; one hundred acres of wheat have been sown, twenty-five acres of corn, five and a half of potatoes, and about four acres of various kinds of vegetables, all of which give promise to fair yield. These Indians are exceedingly industrious, working faithfully and almost as expertly as white people. The younger men do the laborious work and attend to it without murmuring. At present they are camped out, but they express great anxiety to begin to build houses and live in them like white people. As soon as the site of the settlement is decided upon, which will be when a canal that is now being constructed is fully located, the erection of dwellings will be commenced. They declare their intentions to wander about no more, but to lead industrious and respectable lives, at peace with all their fellow creatures, refraining from stealing and all manner of bad practices and abide by the conditions of baptism, which are that they shall cease every species of wrong doing. Elder Hill has baptized about 300 since last spring. The change for the better that has come over these citizens of the mountains indeed is remarkable, which is striking evident to a person passing through their camp at meal times, they will not partake of food until they have returned thanks to the Lord and asked His blessings upon it; they offer up their devotion to the "Great Spirit" morning and evening and attend religious services on Sundays. Paying the strictest attention and behaving with the most scrupulous decorum. They appear to enjoy themselves very much and since their location in the place mentioned, several hundred being camped there, there has never been the slightest indication even of a disposition to quarrel with each other. Such is the simplicity of their faith in God that when there are sick among them, they call for the administration of the ordinance for the sick, where they are almost invariable healed. They labor with an understanding and willingness that shall share in the results, without any inclination to work alone for individual, but for the general welfare. They have their own horses, and plow, sow and do other farm work with readiness. Besides the laboring on the farms they have obtained some means by plowing land for other parties, having done so on the Box Elder Cooperative field.[1]

Other Bands that were starving on government provided reservation land came to find Mormon help as well. But as more and more natives arrived, the white

---

[1] "Civilization among the Indians," *Deseret Evening News*, July 22, 1875.

and non-Mormon population of Corrine became less welcoming.

Sagwitch heard that a group of white farmers had come up with a plan to drive the Shoshone people out of the area, that a telegraph had already been sent to Fort Douglas asking for help against the local Indian tribe. With fresh memories of the Bear River Massacre, Sagwitch feared for his people and for his own life. He had experienced Connor's butchering and was aware of the Army's capabilities. Sagwitch decided to move camp that day. Taking with them what they could, but not wanting the people of Corrine to steal their crops, the women began to destroy all that was left. During the night, Sagwitch and his group began to move north carrying what little they had gathered. Some stopped in Elwood, Utah, fifteen miles north of Corrine, while others headed to Fort Hall, Idaho to stay with relatives and friends. Indians who had been out hunting during the day now returned to find their camp a ghost village. But soon, Sagwitch and his Band realized that they were the victims of a cruel hoax, rumors and betrayal designed to drive the Band away from their land. Though many natives blamed the Mormons for this betrayal, Sagwitch remained true to his faith. In later years as the Indians traveled through Corrine, they would often stop and point out to their young children the place where they were betrayed.

With failures in Franklin, Idaho as well as Corrine, Utah, the only option remaining for the Northwestern Shoshone Band was to once again turn to the LDS Church. George Washington Hill showed tremendous commitment to provide his converts with what he had promised and found land just east of Tremonton, Utah known by the locals as Elwood. Under Hill's direction, Sagwitch and his Band relocated to Elwood in 1976. The Band worked hard and were met with success. A local farmer named Isaac Zundel had also been called as a missionary to the Northwestern Band in 1875, and was assigned to teach the Indians farming and look after their welfare. In the first year, Sagwitch and his Band planted about 100 acres of wheat, 30 acres of corn, 6 acres of potatoes and several acres of vegetables. The harvest went well and everything looked promising once again.

Anticipating that the natives would eventually be forced from their land, Hill returned to Ogden to apply for homestead on behalf of the Shoshone under the 1862 Homestead Act. Over the next several years, the natives successfully built homes and continued to farm, but with decreasingly productive crops. 1877 brought several changes: Brigham Young passed away and Inka-pompy, George Washington Hill to the white man, was released from his missionary call to the Reservationless Indian mission. Through these changes, the farm continued to meet with resistance from the locals, as they had in their previous settlement attempts. Isaac Zundel was appointed director of the Indian Farm in 1878; over the next two years, the Band's efforts were hampered by various government investigations of complaints toward the farm and irrigation failures that haunted its prosperity. With the farm a failure, once again Sagwitch and his Band petitioned the LDS Church for land that was familiar to them, the fertile lands of the Cache Valley. President John Taylor refused the Band's request to return to the Cache

Valley, but offered instead a Church-owned farm just south of Portage, Utah in Box Elder County. The area was in stark contrast to Cache Valley; it was arid with only the occasional sagebrush, but it offered Chief Sagwitch and his Band something that they had always wanted: a land of their own. The Shoshone people were on their way to Washakie. The year was 1880.

Washakie is about three miles from Portage, Utah, six miles south of the Idaho State line. It is located to the west of Interstate 15 and west of the slow-flowing Malad River. The first six families that located at Washakie were those of Sagwitch Timbimboo, Yeager Timbimboo, Soquitch Timbimboo, Hyrum Wongsaw, Da ne po chu and Ammon Pubigee. The LDS Church also bought some land adjacent to the farm from the Merril family. The Shoshone people called the Merrils, "Mooda du der chee." My grandmother said she was not sure why the Indians called them this, as its interpretation means Donkey children.

There were forty public domain allotments on the Washakie Farm that were issued to the Northwestern Band under the authority of three separate acts of Congress: The Citizens Homestead Act of May 30, 1862, The Winnebago Act of 1881 and the Indian Homestead Act of 1884. The Band believed that the LDS Church had given them the land for their permanent location, but the Washakie farm remained Church property and was never owned by the natives. Sagwitch and his Band did not realize that they were only tenants at Washakie, and would only understand this much later when the Band was expected to give up its homes, causing many hard feelings between the Band and the Church.

Under the direction of Zundel and Lorenzo Hunsaker, the Northwestern Band took part in several infrastructure projects including a canal system and sawmills. The Indians operated the mills, a huge success for the natives until the mills were destroyed by fire. The Band believed that the fires were purposely started by jealous white men.

The Band used the money saved from lumber sales and purchased several thousand sheep. Sheep ranching proved to be a positive resource for the natives, earning the Band even more money than the lumber business. One of my grandmother's stories comes from this sheep herding time of the Band. One night the Band noticed a rustler in their sheep pen. The rustler first appeared to be an Indian, but once the thief was caught, it turned out to be a white man dressed like an Indian. The man was arrested, and the Band always referred to him as "White Eyes" when telling the story. But despite initial successes, sheep farming efforts ended in defeat because of disease and theft. A constant repetition of gain and loss became an overarching theme for their experiences with the white man.

Remaining income from their various work adventures allowed the Band to purchase a few large pieces of farming equipment that improved conditions on the farm. They took pride in their new possessions and kept their new equipment in buildings constructed by their own hands and with their own lumber. Over time the Natives had learned to become farmers, carpenters, sheep ranchers, brick masons and lumberjacks. Their desire to build homes of their own became a reality, as the Band built several brick homes in Washakie and Portage, Utah.

The first permanent homes built at Washakie belonged to Soquitch and Towenge Timbimboo.

Initially there was no chapel or meetinghouse in the village to gather and worship, but a large granary at the center of the village served this purpose. The natives would sit on bags of grain while Bishop Zundel stood in the shade of the building and preached. Zundel allowed songs and prayers in the Shoshone language as well as various Shoshone cultural practices, including tribal weddings. In 1881, a large white building was moved to Washakie from one of the nearby farms with the help of Logan contractors working for the Church. This building became the Washakie Ward meetinghouse, recreation hall and first schoolhouse. During these first few years on the Washakie Farm, the Shoshone Band experienced a number of spiritual manifestations which served to strengthen their newfound faith, coupled with genuine commitment as demonstrated in their help with the construction of the Logan temple. Sagwitch and his Band from Washakie donated more than one thousand hours' worth of labor to the sacred site.

Many memories were made at Washakie. The Washakie meeting house served as a dance hall on Friday nights, which not only brought out the Washakie natives but also many white neighbors from Portage and Plymouth, creating many family friendships that continue to this day. Music was a big part of the Shoshone community at Washakie. Every year, the farm children would perform a Christmas program and all of the surrounding communities would be invited attend. The music was performed with the help of the Washakie natives. Thomas Pabaweena and

Washakie White Church House/School house, Washakie, Utah, ca. 1918. Courtesy of Mae Timbimboo Parry

Warren Wongen played the harmonica. Mammie Purdash Wongen sat at the organ and played the latest tunes of the day. Ammon Pubigee and George M. Ward were the callers for the square dancing. Jim Brown and Dick West, who had only one leg, played the fiddle. A Bannock Creek Indian man that attended one of the dances described Dick West saying "As Dick played his fiddle, his empty pant leg was Way-poo-poo-gee-nah," meaning his legless pant leg was swinging to and fro with the beat of the music. The Indians would enjoy themselves all night as they learned to fox-trot, waltz, square dance and two-step.

But not everything at Washakie was appealing. Although there were some structures for housing, many of the Washakie farm natives continued to live in wickiups (a variety of wigwam). A lack of adequate shelter and clean living conditions lead to disease and sickness. Frustrated, Sagwitch and his son Yeager verbalized disgust to Zundel over the running of the farm. A fight ensued with Zundel pushing Yeager, and weapons were drawn. The fight was broken up by an Indian named Da boo cha. After the altercation, Sagwitch packed his belongings and that of the rest of his family and left for Bannock Creek, Idaho. Sagwitch was quoted as saying, referring to Zundel, "white people worship God one day a week, while the Indian worship Him seven days a week." Other families followed their chief and leader including the Hootchews, Grouse Creek Jack and several other families. Sagwitch had a great amount of influence over the natives at Washakie, and his departure caused problems for the Church farm. Sagwitch's Band followed him without question, and little farm work was done in his absence. Sagwitch began to farm at Bannock Creek, the first native to plant and successfully raise a crop of potatoes in the area. He continued to farm in Bannock Creek until his return two years later to Washakie at the request of the Church officials and Zundel. Sagwitch's return to Washakie helped to stabilize the small Indian community.

By 1887, Washakie had become a small city with structures in both the townsite as well as homestead properties owned by individual Indians, acquired in earlier years through the help of George Washington Hill. Sagwitch had worked hard to improve his designated homestead which included a log home, stable and stock yards. Sadly, he died before seeing his ownership properly documented. In 1890, Sagwitch's widow received title to the property. His death is noted on his gravestone in Washakie as 1884, but Sagwitch did not die until March 20, 1887. The documentation of the correct date was likely kept in the Washakie Cooperative store, which was consumed by several fires

Yeager Timbimboo (ca.1848-1937) & Ray Diamond Womenup (ca. 1830-1940), - survivors of the Bear River Massacre. Photo taken ca. 1935, Washakie, Utah. Photo courtesy of Mae Timbimboo Parry.

in 1887 and 1891, completely destroying the store along with a number of crucial historical documents.

In 1912, the Northwestern Shoshone received word that land allotments had opened up on the Fort Hall Reservation in Idaho and the Wind River Reservation in Wyoming. Some of those based in Washakie chose to apply for the allotments, about 160 in total. This represented a significant part of the remaining tribe. Eventually, some obtained allotments and some did not, and more than 100 of the 160 Indians returned to Washakie.

As World War II broke out, most of the Northwestern Shoshones started to leave Washakie to work in defense plants located in Weber and Davis Counties, where the wartime pay was five times greater. My last name, Parry, comes from Joseph Parry, a schoolteacher at the Washakie Day School. Joseph allowed his young son Grant to

1st Shoshone Relief Society at Washakie, Utah, 1918

attend school with the Indian children. Grant Parry and Mae Timbimboo met as five-year-old children and the Parry name comes from their union. My father, Bruce Parry, was born and raised in one of the only remaining houses still standing at Washakie today. It, along with the church/schoolhouse is a national historic landmark, near our graveyard where Sagwitch is buried. My grandmother Mae told me that locals from all around would come to see this "mixed" baby. My grandparents lived at Washakie until my father was twelve and then moved to Clearfield, Utah so that they could work at Hill Air Force Base. Little by little, the once happy Indian community of Washakie was becoming deserted. As the Indian families moved out of their homes, church officials from the farm would burn them down in an effort to "clean up" the area. Several families decided to stay and make a living at Washakie. One summer, as these families were visiting

1st All Native American Bishopric (Shoshone) L to R - Henry Wonsook 1st Counselor, George Ward Service Missionary, Bishop Moroni Timbimboo, Joseph Parry Service Missionary, Jimmy John Neaman 2nd Counselor

relatives in Fort Hall, a local church leader burned the remaining homes with all of their possessions in them. The families returned to find nothing left and wrote letters to church leaders to no avail. There was no response. The Indian village was gone.

The Washakie Ward was officially disorganized on November 24, 1960. The once thriving church farm was sold to the Peterson brothers of Roy, Utah and became a cattle ranch. A white placard at the site once read, "Washakie Indian Reservation." The sign has since been removed. At one time many travelers took time to drive out and visit the Washakie Indians, either to trade deer skins for gloves, moccasins and other beaded artifacts, or simply out of curiosity. Boy Scout Troops would often come and stay for days. I now understand why my father would not let me participate in the Boy Scout program as a kid. He always said, "Boy Scouts are for those kids who are trying to become Indians, and you are already an Indian."

The road sign now reads "Washakie" only. The word "Reservation" is missing, a fact that did not go unnoticed by the Indians. However, one group of dedicated businessmen from Ogden did not forget the Washakie Indians or Chief Sagwitch. The Ogden Pioneer Luncheon Club Chapter of the Sons of Utah Pioneers decided to honor the little Indian village by erecting a monument honoring Chief Sagwitch Timbimboo, a Northwestern Shoshone Chief, and one of the few survivors of the Bear River Massacre. I have seen the monument placed where Sagwitch is buried, and have read the headstone hundreds of times. But even as I read the text today, I notice just how inaccurate most of the narrative seems to be.

SAGWITCH TIMBIMBOO PROMINENT SHO-SHONE CHIEF. BORN 1822 NEAR PRESENT SITE OF BEAR RIVER CITY, BOX ELDER COUNTY, UTAH. DIED MARCH 20,1884 WASHAKIE, UTAH. SON OF BENEANEAR WOOMETADSEGIH. BAPTIZED INTO LDS CHURCH AUG. 1875. GRANDFATHER OF MORONI TIMBIMBOO. BISHOP OF WASHAKIE WARD 1939 TO 1945. ONE OF FEW SURVIVORS OF THE "BATTLE OF THE BEAR RIVER" JANUARY 1863. FIRST BURIAL IN WASHAKIE CEMETERY. ERECTED BY OGDEN PIONEER LUNCHEON CLUB CHAPTER OF SONS OF UTAH PIONEERS. MAY 25, 1963.

The inaccuracy does not upset me, and I do not think the old Chief would be too upset either. It is just one more example of a way of life that has been carefully erased. We are used to that today, but we must work hard to change that trajectory in the future.

CHAPTER 8

Today

My heart is full of gratitude that I have opportunities that generations of my people have prayed for. My grandmother's whole life and purpose was to ensure that the story of her people was heard. As a sovereign Nation, we are making this a reality. It has always been so important to our people that our story be told with our voice and from our unique perspective. This is not because we are looking to have things made right—things cannot be made right, although we should continue that work—but my grandmother and elders always felt that those who sacrificed their lives at Bear River must be heard. As I've said before, their voices cry to us from the dust. The souls of my ancestors peer out from behind my mask of skin and through my memories and efforts, they get to live again.

The massacre at Boa Ogoi is a complex story with many influences from other cultures outside of our own. We did not invite the Mormon Pioneers to this valley, but they came nonetheless. To them, it was their divine destiny; God wanted them to be there, and so they came, with little thought given to who that might hurt or displace. We did not invite those who were seeking gold and other riches to move through our land at will, but they did. Sagwitch himself said that he was fine with the white man seeking all of the gold they wanted, though it belongs

January 29th 2018 Massacre Commeration, Preston, Idaho

to the Indian; all he wanted was to be left alone. But all of these encroachments became our reality and, in the end,, our demise. What my grandmother would want you to know is that we have survived. We have adapted and are thriving in a world that seems so polarized and black and white. We had to adapt to our surrounding environment, or we would have been destroyed. We are just now beginning to blossom as a rose, as some prophecies have said we would. The great Shoshone Chief Washakie stated "Our skins that were once dark because our Father above the clouds had turned his back on us, are now becoming light because His face is towards us once again." Through assimilation, we have been blessed.

It is important that those voices from the past be heard, but it is equally important that the voices from today are heard and respected. We are similar in some ways to other groups whose voices have been marginalized or ignored because of skin color or gender or religion. We have traveled those same roads before, enduring conflict, pain,

Elder Rios Pacheco & Chairman Darren Parry - 150th Anniversary of the Transcontinental Railroad, Promontory, Utah, May 2019

and discrimination. You would think that we would have learned from the mistakes and prejudices from the generations that have gone before, but we haven't. As a little girl, my grandmother was called up to the front of her class and was told to stand on a chair. The white schoolteacher then told the class that she was a dirty little Indian child, and wouldn't amount to anything in this life. We do not hear those same words today, but the message is still the same to some: kill the Indian to save a child.

It wasn't that long ago that Native Americans were not recognized as citizens of the United States. Native Americans were not allowed to vote in all fifty states until 1962. When our children and grandchildren go to school, the history that is taught to them is not their history. They learn about the great Christopher Columbus, and they learn a distorted view of the original Thanksgiving,

Education is the key to our future, Paradise, Utah, May 2016

but little more. When it comes time to learn about their own people, during that one-week period set aside to learn about the Indians, it is usually the Hollywood version of the Red Man and nothing more. This is how our society still wants my people to be viewed, but we say: we have had enough of the sanitized versions of history. It is time for us and all Native peoples to tell their story. Those traditions about our people and those histories carry as much meaning now as they did back then.

I am neither angry nor bitter about the treatment of Native Americans in the past, but I am passionate about making sure that our voice is heard in the future. We want a seat at the table with everyone else and we want to be heard. It is funny that in this day and age that I even have to say this, but we want to be viewed today as equals, because we are equals. We want to be valued and receive recognition of our hard work and efforts. We have no interest in handouts; we want a level playing field and the chance to work every day and earn our keep, because this is what our ancestors did every day of their lives. Every member of the tribe played an important role in its survival. And we have survived!

I have been told by other Native American leaders that we, the Northwestern Shoshone Nation, are not to be taken seriously because we did not have reservation land, and so our experiences are different and our views largely invalid. It's true that we've never been confined to a reservation, and this has also become our biggest blessing. We do not have the same level of problems as found on reservations: drug abuse, alcoholism, suicide and unemployment that can run five times the national average. Reservations are designed to keep us down and dependent. This will never be the life of a Northwestern Shoshone Indian, and to be fair it is not the life of some Native people who have thrived.

When I was young, my grandparents took me to Washakie and show me an old, empty cinder block home that was once theirs. My grandparents told me that my dad was born there, and they had many wonderful memories there. She told me that in 1960, the way of life for her people at Washakie had come to an end. Most of the families had moved away for more lucrative jobs closer to Ogden, Utah. Our people were scattered and disorganized, the result of people leaving for better opportunities or being forced to leave by the burning of their homes. We now had no home base to keep us together, but we were still Indians and proud of our culture and race. One advantage to living on a reservation is that you live together and share a common culture and language. We did not have this when Washakie ceased to be our home. This all changed in 1978 when a few of our tribal elders petitioned the Federal Government to recognize us as a sovereign nation. To meet those requirements, we needed five hundred potential members and a Tribal Constitution. After two years, those requirements were met, and we were federally recognized as a Tribal Nation. This was significant because it allowed us to organize a Tribal Council, set up a government and perhaps equally more importantly, receive federal grant funding. This would allow us to offer our members help with housing, health care and education—many of those same things that we used to have in Washakie. This was a turning point for our tribe. We had an identity again. We never lost hope in who we were as an indigenous people, but now the Government had a responsibility to recognize us and give us the help and respect that we deserve.

Like most things in life, good things did not happen overnight; there were a lot of growing pains in those early days, learning how to manage grant money and spend those dollars appropriately. It has taken time to develop the tribal programs that we have today, but these programs are helping our members in significant ways. Today, our programs are being administered by younger tribal members who have taken advantage of the educational opportunities that the tribe was able to give. They are now returning home to work with our people. Ten years ago, our staff was made up of non-tribal members. There is a sense of pride and accomplishment in being able to give back and serve your people.

Our Housing Authority today manages thirty-seven low income subsidized homes that are rented out to our members in need, to serve our elderly and those trying to get on their feet. The Housing Authority works closely with the Department of Housing and Urban Development to ensure that the grant money is used properly. We have units in Ogden, Brigham City, and Pocatello, Idaho. We also assist first-time home buyers with money for a down payment. We have money set aside for emergency repairs, and we can help tribal members with routine maintenance costs.

Our healthcare services are second-to-none. We no longer solely rely on the Shaman or Medicine Man, even though at times I think that is exactly what we need. We receive grant money from a federal program called Indian Health Services. What makes us unique is that most tribal nations that have reservation land either have a hospital or clinic to service their member's needs. Because we did not move to a reservation, our programs are a little different. In 1980, as part of being federally recognized, we had to select two different counties within the State of Utah where most of our members resided. We were then allotted an amount of money to try and serve the people within that area. To make our dollars stretch further, we require our tribal members to have some kind of primary care coverage, such as private insurance or Medicaid or Medicare. We then serve as a secondary plan to cover any outstanding expenses. We also cover all of our members' prescription costs. Back in the old days, everyone's needs were taken care of by the Band. This is our way to try and do the same.

Patty Tiimbimboo Madsen, Cultural Resource Manager, Massacre Commeration, Preston, Idaho

Education is the key to our future. In the old days, education was all about learning life's lessons that would help you live and survive. Education for our children today is no different and should be the weapon of choice in Indian Country. I like the saying, "give a man a fish and you feed him for a day; teach a man to fish and you feed him for a lifetime." We are teaching our children to fish. We will never write someone a payout check from profits obtained from our tribal business, but we will help our people pay for college education and give them other resources to succeed. I have always believed that the most successful Native Americans today are those who can best balance culture and change. We honor those who have gone before; they are important to us, but we realize that we live in an ever-changing world and we are preparing our youth to change and succeed with it.

Today, we are approximately 550 strong, and we recognize and allow full-bloods to one-eighth blood quantum as members. The government told us that we had to have a blood quantum limit to control our enrollment. Blood

Signing of the purchase of the Massacre Site, January 2018, Preston, Idaho

quantum is the concept and invention of the white man. I believe that amount of Indian blood running through your veins does not make you any more or less of an Indian. Being Indian is an identity engrained in a person from their youth. Being Indian is who you are. It is all of your thoughts, feelings and experiences. I would often hear my grandmother tell complete strangers, "go and ask my grandchildren who they are." The answer was predictable and always the same . . . WE ARE INDIANS!

In January 2018, we were able to purchase 550 acres of the Bear River Massacre Site. It was a huge blessing for my people to obtain this sacred burial ground. Knowing that the spirits of our people lie just beneath the surface makes this a way that we can honor and protect them, and makes owning this land critical. Over the years since the massacre, it has been used as farmland and grazing land. I had the privilege of negotiating this land deal with Ralph Johnson, prior owner of the land. There were many times during this process that I felt discouraged, but I believe that

Concept Drawing of the Cultural Interpretive Center

I felt the influence of my tribal family who had passed on to the spirit world, especially that of my grandmother Mae. I know that doors were opened and hearts were softened because of my ancestors. Ralph Johnson was so kind to us, and I want to thank him and his family for giving us the opportunity of acquiring a piece of ground that means so much to us.

With this land purchase, we will be able to tell our story the way that it needs to be told. We have hired architects to design an interpretive center for this purpose. This will be a place that people can go to and learn for generations to come. It is my hope that as we meet together to tell our story, that everyone can learn from this history.

I have decided that many people have a mental snapshot of native people taken more than 200 years ago and for some reason they want to retain that image. I have always believed that ancient tribal cultures have important lessons to teach the world. Lessons of interconnectedness of all living things and the fact that our very existence is dependent on the world we seem to be destroying. We are not a thing of the past. We are not extinct. Our languages are still strong, ceremonies that we have been

Idaho Governor Brad Little, Boise, Idaho, 2018

conducting since the beginning of time are still being held. Our governments are still surviving and most importantly, we continue to exist as distinct groups in the midst of the most powerful country in the world. But we long to be heard and recognized. We have a culture and history that our troubled world needs that will instill values and ideals that speak to the heart and soul.

There is a layer to history that we don't talk about and we largely ignore. It is the "feelings" that native cultures bring, and it will require us to listen with our hearts. Dreams and spiritual experiences are as much a part of who we are than anything else. As we begin to understand these things, it will transform understanding and appreciation for history. A good friend, Quinn Rollins, said "when we reduce history to just data and we remove the emotion or the spiritual side, we lose some of the humanity that makes history important."

As I have traveled around the country meeting with various tribal nations, I find that we are all in very different

Tribal Council - (L to R) Michael Gross - Secretary, Dennis Alex - Vice Chairman, Jason Walker, Darren Parry - Chairman, Shane Warner - Treasurer, Jeff Parry, Brad Parry, Brigham City, Utah, July 2019

places when it comes to reconciliation. That fact is not surprising to me because I have noticed those same feelings when it comes to my own people. As I have examined the life of Chief Sagwitch I have learned that he was a peacekeeper and one always willing to extend a hand in friendship to those people who wanted something different. He was kind and giving and was often taken advantage of. I am very much like him in that respect. But there are those within my group that are not there yet. There are feelings of resentment and betrayal for the things that have happened in the past. My grandmother was one of those. She had a gentle demeanor but a spirit of unquenchable anger for the things that had happened to her people in the past . . . and that is OK. Her experiences in life and being able to sit at the feet of her grandfather who survived the Bear River Massacre took her perspective down a different path. Not better or worse, just different and I love and respect her for that. It is my hope that we can recognize the mistakes of our forefathers so that we can begin to reconcile our differences. Historian David Lewis said, "history doesn't always affirm us. Sometimes history challenges us to think about an uglier past that we would rather not have. But that is really the power and benefit of history. It connects us to the past. It connects us to our humanity and our inhumanity. And it offers us a way to move forward, to a new relationship, that is a twenty-first century relationship based on respect. Respect for the truth and what happened in that past moment. That is when you get the possibility for reconciliation." Everyone that you meet in this life has a story worthy of being told. What is your story? Your story is equally important. I am happy to say that this is our story and I am grateful that I have been able to share it with you.

Shoshone Prayer

Oh Great Spirit, whose voice I hear in the winds and whose breath gives to all the world, hear me. I come before you, one of your many children. I am small and weak; I need your strength and wisdom. Let me talk in beauty and make my eye even behold the red and purple sunset. Make my hands respect the things you have made, my ears to hear your voice. Make me wise, so that I may know the things you have taught my people, the lessons you have hidden in every leaf and rock. I seek strength not to be superior to my brothers, but to be able to fight my greatest enemy—myself. Make me ready to come to you with clean hands and straight eyes, so when life fades, as a fading sunset, my spirit may come to you without shame.

Author bio

CPSIA information can be obtained
at www.ICGtesting.com
Printed in the USA
FSHW011717020120
65675FS

9 781948 218207